Human Intimacy

ILLUSION & REALITY

Human Intimacy

ILLUSION & REALITY

VICTOR L. BROWN, JR.

Parliament Publishers
Box 25777
Salt Lake City, Utah 84125

Library of Congress Catalog Card Number: 81-80893

ISBN 1-57008-309-6

Second Softcover Printing, 1998

Printed in the United States of America

ACKNOWLEDGMENTS

Many friends and clients have contributed to this book by reading the manuscript and making valuable suggestions and by sharing with me their own struggles with illusion and reality. Their names cannot be printed because it might violate confidentiality. They know who they are and, I trust, also know of my gratitude.

My colleagues Elizabeth James and Ed Lauritzen generously shared their ideas and knowledge of the literature. Thanks also to research assistants Richard Anderson and Ronald Chapman.

Sandra Franck was tireless as typist, researcher, and coordinator of the myriad elements of such a task.

Allen Bergin, friend and colleague, has given crucial counsel and evaluation throughout this project.

My children, each unique, each someone I admire and love, are more a part of this book than they can perhaps know.

Finally, I am unable to express adequately the debt I owe to the inspiration and example of my wife, Mareen. Without her this book could not have been conceived or written.

CONTENTS

PREFACE

The Search for Human Intimacy

Several years ago, Maria* sought counseling from me for a very serious decision. Although her husband rarely failed at anything, he was so troubled by insecurity and anxiety that his pessimism had alienated their children and friends and made life rather tense and difficult. Maria had become strongly attracted to a male friend who offered affection and acceptance. After thorough soul-searching and a rather objective assessment of the situation's pros and cons, Maria decided to repair her marriage and family rather than get a divorce or indulge in an affair, and after several years of difficult but steady effort, she now has seen her marriage bloom. As her husband gained more emotional security—largely from her mature and unthreatening commitment to the marriage—he mellowed considerably. More than ten years later, their marriage is strong, rewarding, and intimate.

Another friend, Richard, had been married for over twenty years. He was skilled at his profession, earned a good income, and enjoyed several hobbies. At one point, due to his illness, his family had suffered fairly severe stress when a business venture failed. Although there were challenges they certainly seemed surmountable, yet he abruptly left his wife and moved in with another woman. Eventually he left this woman for a third. The last I knew he was living alone and isolated from both family and friends.

---

* Throughout the book, all such names and certain identifying details have been changed.

Both of these friends of mine found much encouragement from current views about marriage to "do their own thing" and leave their marriage in search of other loves. Yet Maria chose not to escape from her unpleasant marriage; by that crucial decision, she eventually found happiness, fulfillment, and intimacy in her marriage because she was in a position to change it. Richard escaped from his marriage only to lose intimacy altogether. Both of them needed intimacy. Both of them wanted it. Both of them struggled with decisions about how to find it. Only one of them succeeded.

This book is about intimacy. As a husband, father, and student of human behavior, I have learned that choosing intimacy is a complex and sometimes difficult process. It involves nothing less than choosing reality over illusion, not just in the spectacular watershed decisions of Maria and Richard but day after day, time after time.

While reality may seem difficult to define in every case, I believe that reality is determined by the consequences of our attitudes and behavior. Sometimes those consequences are not apparent for years. Two young couples married the same day may appear equally in love, equally mature, equally happy; yet ten years later the contentment, peace, and pleasure in one home will proclaim the reality of their love while the bickering, mistrust, and exploitation in the other will reveal that their love was an illusion.

Professional experience has taught me to conclude that reality is the process of identifying consequences while illusion is the process of ignoring consequences, denying them, or misinterpreting them. Realities of human intimacy are love, trust, service, sacrifice, and discipline. Opposed to these realities are the glamorous illusions marketed by our society that equate intimacy with an obsession with self, an insistence that every appetite is legitimate and must be gratified, and, most tragic of all, the belief that the laws of human relations can be violated without damaging consequences.

These beliefs are an illusion, not reality. It is an illusion to believe that unkindness, infidelity, and dishonesty will not severely damage a relationship and that a damaged relationship does not cause pain. Many people cling to their illusions for a long time—some for their entire lifetime—but their ability to deny consequences does not prevent the existence of those consequences. Reality demands that we acknowledge the pain and learn from it, but reality also rewards us with consistent access to pleasure as we gain more skill in living effectively.

I do not consider myself a crusader, but I have become increasingly concerned in the last decade as a teacher working with students, as a counselor working with clients, as a bishop in The Church of Jesus Christ of Latter-day Saints (Mormons) working with my congregation, and as a father with growing children—and now a grandfather—about the cynical values I see washing over people who try hard but sometimes seem helpless in the tidal wave. There is a need to affirm in some way that certain crucial values are still there, unmoved by the waves.

To the many people of varying religious or moral beliefs who have chosen values of love, self-respect, and self-discipline already, this volume may help show the magnitude of that choice and the enormous consequences that depend on maintaining it. To those who have chosen other values—or who have accepted the permissive and self-indulgent values that seem prevalent in American society today—this book may help raise some questions or focus some unformed restlessness they may have already felt.

Because of my respect for the earnest searching of ethical people of every persuasion, this book tries to avoid talking about values in specifically religious or scriptural terms, even though my feeling for a loving God is my ultimate foundation and hope for success for every human love and every worthwhile human value. The reader is invited to consider the social trends, research evidence, and clinical experience that have given rise to those feelings, then evaluate their logic and coherence.

The realities of my experiences as a clinical social worker have led me to focus on the nature of human intimacy. My studies of the scholarly and the popular literature on the subject have demanded that I reexamine my own values and education. Much of what I have read has saddened me; much has reaffirmed my hopeful feelings about the resilience and health of human beings.

This experience helped me accept as bedrock reality that at every stage of our life we seek intimacy as urgently as we seek food and drink. We seek our parents' love. We seek friendship. We seek emotional unity in marriage along with physical fulfillment. Out of the love awakened by our children we find ourselves seeking their love even as we give love.

This universal human need is so powerful that we are vulnerable to deception. Loneliness brings a desperation that makes us willing to see almost anyone as desirable, almost any situation as endurable, *if* it holds out the promise of intimacy. Sadly, there are many who would exploit these needs, not only the personal cruelties of the seducer who flatters a lonely woman, the dishonest teenager who "borrows" money from a retarded person eager for friendship, or the woman who lures a family man into adultery just to prove to herself that she can, but also in the impersonal evil of the popular media.

This is not a cry to destroy the television sets of America or impose movie censorship. There is value in its entertainment and purpose in its educative functions. But among media entertainers and media educators are those who manipulate and exploit our human needs without regard for the consequences to society and to individuals.

We might not even be as much concerned about pornography and its limited audience as about counterfeiters—those who use home television, widely sold books, magazines, and movies to sell to the majority of the population superficial and short-term relationships, materialism, and other demeaning views of the human heart and mind. They sell illusion while we starve for reality.

We are also vulnerable from another powerful influence, scientists, particularly social scientists. In our century, many have accepted the scientific search for objective fact as a legitimate successor to the religious search for universal truth. In science, we seek salvation from pollution, hunger, and poverty. Increasingly, the social scientists assert that they have answers to human needs; and, as someone trained by social scientists, I know that most of them are sincere people, using their skills to help and heal, seeking more effective answers in their research.

Yet confusion, disagreement, and conflict characterize almost every field, assault almost every premise, and challenge almost every conclusion. To expect unanimity of values or universal answers is to ask something that is simply not possible. Science, particularly social science, is a systematic way of reducing ignorance. It takes small, careful, and very constricted steps. The grand sweep of human history and the life-and-death struggles of the human heart are not subject to scientific analysis. To believe that science can mandate, enthrone, or demolish values like love, respect, and discipline on the basis of laboratory experiments is to accept illusion. When one study says that divorce helps children escape an unhappy situation and another says it permanently damages them, it is not possible that both can be correct —although it is possible that both are wrong or only partly right.

My intent should be made clear. It is my hope that the reader will share my conclusions after examining his or her realities and illusions about human intimacy. This is not intended to be a neutral book.

The reader should be a person who expects data and evidence but who also knows that statistics can be used to support almost any opinion. The reader should be active, carrying on an internal discussion with the book, even an argument where appropriate.

Those looking for easy recipes for intimacy will be disappointed. This is not a marriage handbook, not a handy ten-step guide to fulfilling friendship, and not a weekend change-your-life program. Think of it rather as a discussion with a committed friend, a clinician, a respecter of science, an appreciative fan of some of the entertainment media, a husband who is learning in midlife some of the lessons of human intimacy that would have been better known as a teenager, a father concerned about the consequences for six children who could be harmed by the illusions of intimacy rather than blessed by its realities, and a grandfather, loving a generation that he can only briefly touch.

Human behavior results when a person believes enough to act. But belief is not enough to identify reality. A woman can believe that a man loves her; but if his behavior hurts her repeatedly, she must reexamine that belief. Seeking reality, trying to avoid illusion, we must be willing to scrutinize our beliefs in the light of consequences.

My personal beliefs about human intimacy are firmly grounded in principles enunciated by God and Jesus Christ. However, it would be a short book indeed if I just stated my values, for I would simply cite key scriptures. I prefer rather to open the discussion to popular and professional ideas about intimacy, using the tools of logic, reason, and scientific debate to examine the consequences of those beliefs.

Through such an exercise, a person tends either to fall back on uninformed belief or to move ahead to informed belief, pro or con. That is why the reader's active participation is invited. Acting upon informed belief, I believe that the goal of seeking and finding benevolent intimacy with oneself, family, and friends can be better achieved.

At different times in my life, despite an underlying commitment to religious values, I have subscribed to cultural values that have defined success as college degrees, impressive salaries, or dazzling public performances. There is nothing wrong with these values in themselves, but sometimes they have obscured the homely but unrelenting reality that truly superb achievement in treating family and associates with warmth and kindness is the most demanding and the most rewarding of all human ventures.

Many people are successful outside their homes and justify neglecting their families because of the "good work" they are doing at the office, at church, or in civic affairs. As someone who has traveled that road, I believe that there is a better work. As a counselor, I have heard the lonely testaments of clients and friends who would have gladly traded public success—their parents' or their spouse's, their child's, or their own—for warm, unqualified private tenderness within the walls of their own home.

The decision is seldom either-or. We can have success in both places but we cannot give both equal priority. Reality, that exercise in consequences, urges that we put human relationships first.

Saying so does not make it happen. We are left with the real struggle to achieve real intimacy. The mind is a powerful yet vulnerable tool in this struggle. Our mind, if it experiences enough confusion or pain, may seek extraordinary and uncertain paths which turn out to be illusions, in preference to tangible yet often ordinary realities. Some seek heaven only to find hell. The poet Milton, in *Paradise Lost*, understood the power of the human mind and will to overcome hellish circumstances and the perverse tendency to give up heavenly circumstances:

> The mind is its own place, and in itself
> Can make a Heaven of Hell, a Hell of Heaven.
> (Bk. 1, lines 254-55.)

You, the reader, are invited to use this book in the strenuous yet exhilarating search for intimacy in which we are all engaged. It is offered by a fellow seeker.

CHAPTER ONE

The Illusions and Realities of Human Intimacy

This book speaks of the ideal but not of the impossible. It speaks of facing reality and rejecting illusion. It sees intimacy as a broad, deep term, not a synonym for sexuality.

Achieving intimacy is a demanding activity and this book does not minimize these demands. No one has ever been motivated by the slogan "Onward and Sideways!" or "Progress through Mediocrity!" Intimacy is one of the highest ideals of the human heart and, as such, deserves the most exceptional efforts.

Principles of Intimacy

The lives of most people are histories of their search for intimacy, of their attempts to be socially, physically, and emotionally close to others. It includes the total offering and the total acceptance of whole people, not the superficial interaction of fragments, whether in a sexual encounter or in cautious comments about the weather.

Here are some principles of intimacy which this book discusses.

1. Each human being must establish his or her own identity, for each of us is unique, unlike any other person. Without this identity, there is no whole person to offer to another, no whole person to accept the gift of intimacy from another.

2. Identity begins with gender, being male or female; but individual role definitions (what *kind* of male or female) are unlimited in potential.
3. Becoming intimate with others requires us to develop a repertoire of relationship skills based upon our identity and role.
4. Intimacy expands and deepens within marriage and the family more than in any other relationship.
5. Intimacy is an enduring relationship between whole people. It includes communion with one's innermost self and union with others in social-emotional, mental, physical, and spiritual ways.

Intimate relationships are deeply and profoundly nourishing. The adults I know who are happy are a mixed lot with all kinds of vocations and all kinds of incomes; they belong to many different religions and have many different hobbies. What they all have in common is a profound peacefulness at their centers. They give love wholeheartedly and receive it joyously. People like them and like to be around them. When they succeed they clearly enjoy it. When grief occurs in their lives, they mourn. They have personal integrity. They value their time yet are willing to spend a good portion of it in serving others. They value their possessions yet are willing to share them with others. They make mistakes and admit them honestly, accepting the consequences and structuring their lives to avoid repeating them. They respect themselves and others. They are profoundly in touch with reality and the consequences show in their lives.

Reality has had an undeservedly bad press, for we tend to think of it as unpleasant. C. S. Lewis's popular *Screwtape Letters* has one devil pointing to another:

> You will notice that we have got them [human beings] completely fogged about the meaning of the word "real." They tell each other, of some great spiritual experience, "All that *really* happened was that you heard some music in a lighted building"; here "real" means the bare physical facts, separated from the other elements in the experience they actually had. On the other hand, they will also say, "It's

> all very well discussing that high dive as you sit here in an armchair, but wait till you get up there and see what it's *really* like"; here "real" is being used in the opposite sense to mean not the physical facts (which they know already while discussing the matter in armchairs), but the emotional effect those facts will have on a human consciousness. . . . Your patient, properly handled, will have no difficulty in regarding his emotion at the sight of human entrails as a revelation of reality and his emotion at the sight of happy children or fair weather as mere sentiment.[1]

Lewis has, by this ironic means, put his finger on one of our society's problems, the prevalence of illusion, especially about our own nature as human beings. One of our tasks during mortality is to learn to recognize and use reality. We think of reality as unyielding and so it is—happily so. Reality demands that we acknowledge the sources of our happiness and demands that we recognize the sources of our misery. Once these realities are acknowledged, we can choose to behave as we like, but the consequences are inescapable.

A simple reality which is ignored at a terrible price is that most human misery can be prevented by wise and disciplined living. Physical disease, for example, offers some dramatic instances. Due to improved hygiene, tuberculosis deaths decreased from two hundred per hundred thousand population to twenty between 1900 and 1950. That was *before* effective anti-TB drugs were available.[2] Cancer of all types could be dramatically reduced if people would not take known carcinogenic substances into their bodies.[3]

Instead of self-restraint, however, our society indulges excessive appetites and seeks excessive cures. We seem to believe that substances ranging from Alka-Seltzer to penicillin can cure the consequences of unwise behavior. Millions of dollars are spent on "cures" for alcohol abuse and venereal disease. They are not spent to teach us to avoid liquor or sexual adventure.

The same principles seem to hold true in areas of emotional health. Lasting, rewarding intimacy with self and others is the result of wise and disciplined living, not the quick and easy indulgence of appetite.

Let's look at some case studies. Annette had suffered for years with an inattentive, workaholic husband. Her self-esteem was eroding from loneliness. In desperation, she challenged his competing interests and learned the unwelcome fact that she had played a part in making work more attractive than being home. Honestly her husband admitted his own unwillingness to spend the time and energy on his marriage that he knew it would take. At this point, they considered divorce. But gradually they were able to admit that they had both been desperately lonely and needed each other. As they learned how to recognize and respond to each other, mainly by kind but candid talking, they became intimate allies rather than opponents.

As a second example, a colleague and I once gathered personal histories of five women who appeared to be coping rather well with life. They enjoyed their marriages, got along reasonably well with their children, and had weathered emotional and financial storms without capsizing. In every case, each woman recalled a childhood that included a consistently affectionate mother and a reassuring father. Chats during work, vacations spent together, serious talks about adolescent heartaches, and support in trying out new talents and skills were part of that pattern. The sum of their memories was that mother and father cared —even though several of the parents had serious personal problems of their own.

In contrast was Linda, who checked into an out-patient mental health unit so regularly that the staff regarded her as an old friend. She was diagnosed as schizophrenic. Her husband's financial irresponsibility was so complete that Linda, after bearing the verbal abuse of bill collectors day after day, took periodic relief in madness. Asked why she tolerated his behavior and never demanded that he change, she said in mild surprise, "He loves me." She lived daily with the results of that wishful illusion.

Intimacy's Counterfeits

There is no one name for the counterfeits of intimacy since

they often masquerade under the honorable names of love, friendship, and romance, debasing these terms by their very use of them. Although the sad instances of such illusions appear all too often in the lives of ordinary people, I would like to suggest characteristics of illusory intimacy as they appear most frequently in the media. In every instance, the ultimate test of illusion and reality is the long-term consequences, but there are some "reality checks" that are helpful much sooner in eliminating some damaging, dangerous choices.

Illusions are, by their very nature, incomplete portrayals of reality. If they were complete, they would *be* real since reality includes both negative and positive, pleasure and pain. Among the important characteristics of illusions about human relationships are: (1) Illusions deal with fragments of human beings, not with whole human beings. (2) Illusions deny the consequences of human behavior. (3) Illusions deal in indulgence, not discipline.

Fragmentation

A man glimpsing a neighbor woman might be aroused by her body and try to seduce her. Encountering an icy refusal, the shock of her children, or the anger of her husband would teach him that his fantasies were an illusion. On the other hand, if he were to share gardening tips, social activities, and a mutual love for summer sunsets with this woman, he might well develop a real though nonsexual intimacy with a whole person—a neighbor, a talented human being, a wife, a mother, and a daughter.

Fragmentation enables its users to counterfeit intimacy. Such emotionally crippled people as voyeurs, child molesters or rapists act out their fragmented illusions. They cannot relate to a whole person, but mentally or physically use parts of another's body to gratify their appetite for power.[4]

If we relate to each other in fragments, at best we miss full relationships. At worst, we manipulate and exploit others for our gratification. Sexual fragmentation can be particularly harmful because it gives powerful physiological rewards which, though illusory, can temporarily persuade us to overlook the serious deficits in the overall relationship. Two people may marry for physical gratification and then discover that the illusion of union collapses under the weight of intellectual, social, and spiritual incompatibilities.

It is ominous for our future that a generation is being raised on television fare which teaches that a "loving" relationship can be developed in five days on an ocean liner cruising the Pacific or over a weekend while living on an island devoted to fantasy. Our children may know that relationships take longer to develop, but still they sometimes wonder if there isn't a separate category of reality called "falling in love" where the ordinary rules are suspended, when something magical and reality-defying occurs. If they do suspend the rules this is where heartbreak begins, but it is never shown on cruise boats or islands of fantasy. Through fragmentation, the larger matter of human intimacy is reduced to the smaller part of sex.

In other areas of human relations, fragmentation becomes a tactic to reduce complex social-emotional situations to the lowest common denominator, the quickest, least challenging way of relating to self or others. An inquisitive child is ordered to be quiet. A wife is treated as a house servant. A widowed mother is bundled off to a retirement colony except for Christmas visits. In intimate human relationships, alienation replaces acceptance as interactions become restricted, and ignorance replaces understanding. As with a broken work of art, we glimpse a small though intriguing fragment and do not know the pleasure of the entire masterpiece.

Sexual fragmentation is particularly harmful because it is particularly deceptive. The intense human intimacy that should be enjoyed in and symbolized by sexual union is counterfeited by sensual episodes which suggest—but cannot deliver—acceptance, understanding, and love. Such encounters mistake the end for the means as lonely, desperate people seek a common denominator which will permit the easiest, quickest gratification.

Denying Consequences

When the media present violent, crude, and bizarre behavior *without also presenting the consequences* then everyone suffers. We would not exclude unpleasantness from literature or entertainment and present only "pretty" messages. Such thinking would replace the Old Testament with Harlequin romances. But the record in the Old Testament of David's passion for Bathsheba does not claim that love justifies all. Instead it unsparingly presents the ugly consequences of that self-indulgence for both of them.

In contrast, the twentieth century media, including "real" shows such as sports, delete the hostilities of intense competition, avoid documenting injuries, and camouflage the personalities of some of the people who play violent games for a living. The screen shows the end of the heavyweight fight, but not the dozens of stitches in the loser's face. The racing car crashes, but we see only its toy-like tumbling, not the broken body and charred flesh of the driver.

From the football sidelines the new team psychiatrist witnesses his first game and reports something the home viewers never see:

> I closed my eyes. When I got up the courage to open them, I saw the result of my first on-the-field NFL play. Banaszack was down on his back in front of me. His mouth was twitching peculiarly. His eyes were closed. Rick Redman, our linebacker who got Banaszack, was down, too. On his right side and holding his left shoulder and whimpering quietly. I was overwhelmed. I wanted to run away. . . . My nervous system never really recovered from that first hit until close to the end of the game.[5]

Is it surprising that today's generation succumbs to the illusion that a human being is a thing which, within seconds or minutes, rebounds from body-breaking or heart-breaking assault and overcomes physical and emotional trauma?

One of the reasons why couples divorce is that they believe that the consequences will be better than remaining married.

Sometimes this is true. Mavis E. Hetherington, analyzing the consequences of divorce for children, concludes that "a conflict-ridden family is more deleterious to family members than is a stable home in which parents are divorced," partly because "a rejecting or hostile parent is more detrimental" than an absent one. Even so, she warns, "most children experience divorce as a difficult transition, and life in a single-parent family can be viewed as a high-risk situation for parents and children."[6] Another reputable study of the consequences of divorce for children is Wallerstein and Kelly's study of sixty divorced families. Five years after divorce, 28 percent of the children approved, 42 percent neither approved nor disapproved and 30 percent disapproved. This rather balanced profile after five years contrasts with the first year after divorce when 75 percent of the same children strongly opposed the divorce. Wallerstein and Kelly concluded that divorce should remain an "option to adults who are locked into an unhappy marriage," although their findings were "somewhat graver than expected." They comment hauntingly, "Hardly a child of divorce we came to know did not cling to the fantasy of a magical reconciliation between his parents. . . . The faithfulness of so many youngsters to their predivorce families was unsettling." They also reported enormous efforts the divorced or remarried parents made to help their children adjust.[7]

Yet surely a third alternative is conspicuous by its absence. Why are the consequences of healing a troubled marriage and acquiring the skill to parent in a disciplined, loving way left unexplored? My own counseling experience teaches me that this course of action has a positive effect that extends for generations and has the most desirable consequences of all: avoiding the pain of remaining in a troubled marriage and avoiding the inevitable pain of divorce, which Lee Salk, himself divorced, characterizes as "undoubtedly one of the greatest stresses a human being can experience. It is second only to the distress suffered from the loss of a loved one through death. . . . In fact, anyone approaching divorce with calm and composure is probably not facing the situation realistically. . . . Divorce sets up circumstances that are so disorganizing that everyone subjected to it feels overwhelmed and wonders how he or she can make it through."[8]

It is a requirement of intimacy to understand basic cause and effect in human relations and to move toward desired consequences by making correct decisions. *Behavior has consequences.*

One interesting study by Masters and Johnson interviewed a group of "swingers" (couples who share spouses), who claimed that there was no jealousy and that outside sexual partners actually enlivened the marriage relationship. A follow-up report twelve months later revealed that some of the couples had divorced, others were impotent, and that all were reevaluating their relationships. Only one couple reported a stable relationship and they had stopped "swinging."[9] They had discovered, in other words, that they could not deny the consequences of indulgence.

It is hard for me to watch portrayals of sophisticated adultery on television, with husband and wife exchanging urbane chit-chat about infidelity, when in the clinic I deal with real long-term effects: a husband must be legally restrained after threatening to kill his wife's lover. Neither couple divorces, but all of them, including the children, struggle for years to resolve bitter feelings of betrayal, anger, and mistrust. Furthermore, both families are financially devastated by lawyers' fees, lost employment, and moving expenses when the situation becomes so inflammable that a new location seems necessary. The indulgent person and his victims must live with the real consequences of his behavior, just as the disciplined person and his beneficiaries live with the benevolent realities of his.

Self-Indulgence

The American dream has, to many of us, meant being able to gratify our hunger for food, power, wealth, and emotional satisfaction. The "consumption-drugged" American averages using a barrel of oil every six days, an uninhibited selfishness that seriously affects other nations: 55 percent of Western Europe's energy comes from oil and 75 percent of Japan's.[10] Our affluence is both the envy and concern of the world. As a nation, we try to solve problems by manipulating our environment to accommodate our habits, the illusion of indulgence.

Restraint, either fiscal or sexual, is viewed with disdain. One widely used text asserts that "virtually all boys masturbate" but adds reassuringly that "women who have never masturbated are not necessarily pathological."[11] Masters and Johnson, world-renowned sexologists, approvingly describe "ambisexuals" who, because of their technical skill and very lack of emotional involvement, achieve orgasm 100 percent of the time in their sexual encounters. These researchers concluded that such physical success gave ambisexuals the advantage over heterosexual men or women because this "absence of sexual preference" also means an absence of "sexual prejudice" which, they claim, is "a cornerstone that supports any number of other social biases." These "privileged" individuals, according to Masters and Johnson, may be pointing the way for society at large.[12] Such messages are disturbing.

Furthermore, even while Masters and Johnson hold up the ambisexual as a model, they report of telling emotional sterility. Ambisexuals seldom show any interest in "a committed relationship" or feel "affection" for their parents and siblings. Johnson and Masters conclude bleakly, "By free admission the lifestyle of the ambisexual is a lonely one."[13]

An expensive pricetag on indulgence is growing sexual disinterest, "probably the most prevalent of all the sexual dysfunctions," according to one researcher.[14] This is the last consequence that those who worked to remove the "rigidity" and "repression" of a Judeo-Christian values system would have predicted. It would not, however, surprise anyone in a position to experience the increasingly subtle and sophisticated pleasures of a secure long-term relationship in contrast to the monotonously similar beginnings of repeated promiscuity. Reality has simply collided with illusion.

When impossible models of performance are held before us, we tend to reject them and turn away, whether they be a perfectly set holiday table, a 4.0 grade point average in school, a family whose children never disobey, or the fantasy view of physical intimacy that is unlimited in its variety and complete in its ecstasy. Common sense or despair or both tend to "turn us off." Propaganda to the contrary, all marriage counselors know men who are immobilized by a wife's aggressiveness and women who are unresponsive to physical contact separate from affection and consideration.

The message, though unpopular, is clear. Unlimited gratification leads not to increased pleasure but to decreasing satisfaction, to greater boredom, and to diminished pleasure. Paradoxically, the price of pleasure is restraint. Homely examples from daily experience confirm that great pleasures are purchased at the price of little ones, and long-term satisfaction comes from short-term sacrifice.

Self-discipline makes it possible for a teenager to put money aside for her college tuition rather than buying another pair of designer jeans. It enables sleep-starved parents to take turns rocking a sobbing baby until the antibiotics can work on its ear infection. It enables a widower to weep through the lonely hours of the night without dulling his pain with drugs and to do his work the next day without hiding in that same pain from his responsibilities.

The self-disciplined person does not exercise restraint as punishment but as a means to an end. A woman controls her appetite because she likes the way her body feels when her weight is down. An engaged couple refrain from premarital sex, not to deprive themselves of physical pleasure but because they respect the rights and privileges that the marriage vows will give them. A father is calm in the face of his teenage daughter's stormy insistence that she use the family car, not because he does not feel impatient but because he knows that getting angry will neither solve the problem nor help their relationship.

Intimacy and appetite are not enemies. Indeed, they attend the creation and nurturance of our bodies. Whether at mother's breast, cuddling in father's arms, playing with siblings or friends, or courting, the universal human theme is a search for intimacy often fueled by emotional and physical appetite.

It is illusory, however, that we can always gratify our appetites quickly, easily, and completely. It is equally illusory that we cannot enjoy our appetites while living a disciplined, moderate life.

The Requirements of Intimacy

My experience suggests that intimacy has two main components: *risk* and *commitment.* The counterfeits of intimacy parade the illusion that nothing is risked but a little inconvenience in establishing a new relationship and that commitment can be contracted by a mutual agreement to service each other's needs, ending whenever either person wants to terminate the relationship.

The reality is that risk exists because we grant another person the power to bring us joy or pain. We begin intimacy hoping for joy but we open our hearts enough to be hurt if it fails. Commitment goes beyond risk, for it is our decision to care even if the other person ceases to care for us. A father commits his heart and his energy to children who frequently resent that care when it manifests itself in discipline.

Risk and commitment both require decisions. Those decisions allow two people to create love rather than "fall in" love, a phrase that fatally advertises its own abandonment of responsibility to forces beyond its control. Furthermore, they both require the difficult, long-term decision to expose ourselves to another person so that we can be known, matched by the decision to accept that other person in his or her own wholeness.

Perhaps the single most frequent pattern of troubled relationships has been that they are based upon the quickest, easiest processes. It requires no extraordinary wisdom to see that if a man and woman come together primarily because they attract each other physically that there will be little to maintain the relationship once the glamorous fantasies have the opportunity of meeting less-than-perfect reality. It takes comparatively little thought or discipline to have sexual intercourse. Eroticism is probably the lowest common denominator in human relations because it requires only appetite, the opportunity to gratify it, and normal physiological functioning. Its demands on the intellect and the heart are low. So are its consequent rewards when it is the basis of a relationship.

Time is the ultimate test of commitment, both in the lives of individuals and in our culture. The few decades of "liberation" our society has experienced are too short to make extravagant conclusions on. In contrast, the longterm results of deciding for intimacy rather than indulgence only become more impressive. One interesting example is the study of Framingham, Massachusetts, a community characterized by general social stability and personal emotional health. It was first surveyed in 1948. Over twenty years later, in 1970, Framingham, a community of 65,000, was still characterized by stable marriages, religious involvement, high employment, effective schools, and so forth. Related consequences were a very low coronary disease rate, a fifteen percent lower death rate than the national average, only three percent illegitimate birth rate, no homicides, four suicides, and a .001 divorce rate.[15]

Even though the factors behind such statistics are no doubt complex, the myriad daily decisions to be decent, disciplined, and respectful of others are also manifest. Surely as a society we have a stake in sustaining intimate relationships and reducing divorce and violent death. And surely it is good to face clearly the consequences of intimate human acts.

Risk

The emotional risk of a relationship is real. The serious lover stands to either gain a great deal or lose a great deal. A relationship overwhelmingly engages the emotions, draws from them, feeds them, creates new ones, and requires the reinterpretation of old ones. Relationships need not be turbulent and dramatic—the stuff of which soap operas are made—but if they are satisfying, they are richly emotional.

The fact is that an emotionally healthy and emotionally well-nourished person is as much able to undertake strenuous emotional activity as the physically healthy person can undertake physical activity. And ordinary living places extraordinary demands on our emotional systems. All of us will experience the loss of someone close. Few of us will not experience the anxious risk of waiting beside a sickbed. The birth of a baby is a joyful event that can bring along with it gnawing concern for the mother's health, the baby's health, the effect of this new arrival on the other children, a change in the couple's relationship, and even devastating post-partum depression. Few parents will not experience the heartwringing passage of hours while a toddler is lost, while a grade-schooler's x-rays are being developed, or while a teenager, who left the house in defiance, wanders about on a dark night. These events, these risks, underscore the point that family living is not for emotional weaklings.

The positive emotions are equally strong: the passion of shared attachment, the utter trust built up over decades of marriage, the child whose victory is not complete until she shares it with her parents, the son who brings his adolescent uncertainties to his father in the knowledge that his sensitive pride will not be wounded, and the outpourings of tenderness at moments when the feelings of mutually shared love, commitment, and belonging are reaffirmed.

Yet our emotional health is under attack from the media in this area too. I am not talking only of the shallow and frequently silly models of family life that appear on the screen (who wants to celebrate a twentieth wedding anniversary if you're married to Archie or Edith Bunker?) in contrast to the cool, unattached glamour of the fast-driving, hard-hitting, easy-loving singles. What concerns me more is broader and more pervasive, a systematic and subtle detachment of accurate emotional responses from events. It is essential to true intimacy that our emotions be appropriate to our behavior, yet the media denies it, in part by its suggestion that criminals and police can exchange body-battering blows one minute and clever quips the next. Worse, the very form of television, by fragmenting drama with commercials, demands that we also fragment our emotional response. We do not seem designed as human beings to be able to switch emotions off and on at will. Instead we become disengaged—and we stay that way to avoid risk.

For example, in *Holocaust,* an NBC docu-drama aired 11-13 September 1979, one Nazi officer reminds another: "Remember, Colonel, if you kill one hundred Jews, it's then easier to kill a thousand, then ten thousand. . . ." The break for commercials features aspirin, toothpaste, arthritis treatments, and dog food. Then actual footage from Nazi documentaries shows soldiers machine-gunning people in mass trenches, with a closer segment showing a mother holding a child in her arms as the soldier aims his rifle at them. A second commercial break includes felt-tip pens advertised by a laughing man, brassieres, and aspirin. We should not be able to accept such incongruity!

We are—it seems beyond belief to write it—entertained by the agony of our brothers and sisters. Nightly TV news invades the mourning of survivors, demanding statements for "viewers." Desensitized, we respond with uncritical interest. A student at an elite university, a leader of the future, arranges for the death of his unborn child in an illegal operation that will risk the life of its mother. We applaud him for being "convincing" and reach for a sandwich while the sponsor assures us that our pet will be healthy if it eats the right dog food.

Is it possible to overestimate the psychic and moral loss from being able to witness human suffering without feeling pain as other than an aesthetic experience? Is it not logical that such insensitivity also reduces our capacity for joy? Will the products of inventive minds and capable hands chill and numb our hearts?

As another example, nothing may so completely demonstrate the way inappropriate emotions have become acceptable as the way Jesus Christ is treated by the media in our nominally Christian society. Most people are too conscious of the feelings of other cultures to entertain them with mocking references to Mohammed or to ridicule Jewish sacred practices. Yet these same people use Christ's name to express annoyance, humor, surprise, and anger. To millions of people, the name of Christ is the name of a real person and recalls a relationship of special intimacy. Yet these tender feelings are repeatedly violated by the insensitivity and disrespect of others who make the person of Jesus an object of ridicule and his very name a curse.

This discussion, though it has drawn some examples from the media, is not primarily an analysis of its shortcomings. It is, however, an assertion that our society, in accepting and fostering the values portrayed by much of the media, is engaged in the systematic destruction of its ability to recognize, nurture, and risk intimate relations. As police and social workers know, there are terrible, even unspeakable, violations of the human body, heart, and mind. Nothing in real life is entertaining about these tragedies. Humorous or profane attempts to entertain with these themes are jarringly inappropriate. Real people in real crises weep, suffer, and plead for healing peace. It is the greatest of illusions to assume otherwise. Serious commitment in a real relationship—a friendship, a marriage, parenthood—holds forth the promise of great joy and the risk of great pain.

Commitment

One does not "fall into" commitments. They are the purposeful, intentional decisions of a mature and disciplined person who engages himself or herself to act in a certain way over a given period of time. To some extent, a commitment is unilateral and in many ways it is unconditional. The commitment of a parent to a child takes place at a time when the child is incapable of acting for himself or of offering very much in return, ideally before the child is born. The commitment of husband and wife, at least in religious ceremonies, involves a public promise to the institution of marriage itself or to the God who is being asked to recognize and sanctify that relationship. It is far from being a private arrangement between two consenting adults.

In contrast is the contract arrangement that governs a surprising number of marriages and even parent-child relationships. They are tense and wary alliances: "We'll stay married unless it becomes unfulfilling." "You're part of this family as long as you get good grades and don't hang out with the wrong kids." It is a modern narcissism, the socially approved exploitation and manipulation of others. Its chief value is gratification. Its chief satisfaction demands collaborators and it woos them artfully, not to enhance their lives but to exploit them for self-focused purposes. In such a contract, love is irrelevant. Civility is a sometimes useful means for achieving a selfish end. Sacrifice is incomprehensible.

In the law, this is known as *quid pro quo.* Political philosophers call it the social contract. Marriage counselors refer to 50-50. Sex researchers Masters and Johnson refer to "my turn-your turn." These can all be summed up as "yours-mine," meaning "You give me my gratification and I'll give you yours."

This apparently logical maxim of effective social relations is generally accepted as a sound basis for human relationships. In reality, it is a classic illusion which seriously distorts our understanding of the whole matter of intimacy. "Yours-mine" guarantees certain results but, fatally, it never transcends the original agreement nor ever understands that the whole can be greater than the sum of the parts. Like children on a seesaw, the partners never exceed the limits of the contract unless one jumps off, which then injures the other. In "yours-mine" relationships, guaranteed minimal commitment is negotiated ahead of time, thus reducing certain risks but also reducing many rewards. The seesaw partners never soar like those in the swings, one seated and the other pushing, their unequal but combined energies occasionally risking a great fall if careless, but most of the time reaching exhilarating heights.

The language of "yours-mine" is *partners, encounters, rights, assertiveness, despair, illusion.* The language of "us" is *companions, sharing, responsibilities, patience, joy, reality.* One is a grand illusion, the other a grand reality.

In a publication devoted to religion and health, an editorial advocates temporary relationships such as trial cohabitation and short-term marriage as solutions to today's intimate challenges:

> But not forever, not for all time, not for eternity. After all, who can tell about eternity?
>
> The more we ponder this kind of marital union [temporary, short-term], the more modest, sensible, and humane it seems. Those who make such commitments are relieved from the awful burdens of a loyalty that leaves no room for change or even for growth in experience and maturity. They can turn their attention to the important task of making the relationship good for now and for a probable future, trusting that if the seeds of mutual love and shared understanding are carefully nourished now, they will grow and flourish. . . .
>
> The "forever" commitment is probably most dangerous to human growth and the development of constructive wisdom for survival in the realm of religion or in science, philosophy, or social values.[16]

This short-term expediency clashes with my own experience and with virtually every counseling experience I have had. One couple, Jim and Marsha, had tentatively decided to divorce but assessed the investment they had in each other and concluded that to start over with someone else would be a greater risk than working it out with each other. Beginning with relatively little commitment to each other but with a great deal to their children and to the institution of marriage, they spent the next twelve years, working and working hard on their marriage. By that time they had grown to be one, to be richly and deeply intimate in all ways. Yet I have seen other couples who were too impatient to give their relationship twelve months—sometimes not even twelve days.

Unreliable Information About Intimacy

Much of our information about marriages, families, and the root situations that foster intimacy comes from the research explosion in the behavioral sciences. This branch of the sciences has benefited from the general esteem in which science is held, yet I am deeply troubled by some of the illusions from that esteem. Social science is not a religion. Its conclusions are not revealed truth. Nor is it an exact science. All science is a systematic exploration of ignorance, an honorable but uncertain enterprise. And social science is one of the more uncertain cousins. The vaunted "objectivity" of science is vulnerable enough when forces of nature and physical properties are being studied. It becomes fragile indeed when a subjective social scientist studies the subjectivity of other people.

The pioneering psychoanalyst Sigmund Freud is an example. Much of his work, though presented as science, was actually creative and literary. Biographer Peter Drucker points out that "Freud was deeply hurt by any hint that his theory was poetry and not science . . . [yet] Freud was a very great artist, probably the greatest writer of German prose in this century." Drucker also quotes novelist Thomas Mann, who on Freud's eightieth birthday called psychoanalysis "the greatest contribution to the art of the novel."[17] Another biographer, Frank Sulloway, recently presented the troubling proposition that the theories of psychoanalysis may be "the most stupendous intellectual confidence trick of the twentieth century."[18]

Freud was unquestionably brilliant, but how reliable are his prescriptions for intimate behavior when we include the facts that he never resolved conflicted relations with his father, ambiguous feelings about his Viennese-Jewish culture, and a distrust of his own sexuality that eventually led to an asexual relationship with his wife. We should not demand that a teacher must be perfect before he or she can teach, but our confidence in how easily some problems will give way before a teacher's sweeping prescriptions must, perforce, be cautious.

The same reservations hold as we contemplate the influential philosophers and savants who shaped the scientific method and educational process that has molded the current education of behavioral scientists. Many of those philosophers, eloquently constructing models for life's meaning, were unable to establish healthy, intimate relationships in their own lives. Perhaps their minds were moved by their hearts' private pain; but while they soared intellectually, they failed emotionally. Jean-Jacques Rousseau, the voice of the common man, bitterly lamented his failure to cope with being a husband and a father.[19] Christian existentialist Soren Kierkegaard died young and unmarried, refusing to marry the one woman he had loved because he did not want to burden her with his melancholy life.[20] Friedrich Nietzsche led a very lonely life and died insane.[21]

However, we all know and speak better than we act. The private failures of these men do not lessen their contributions. Their disservice to us is not that they were troubled or aloof but that they—or their disciples—implied they knew something which, in fact, they did not. With finite ideas, which even their finite experience contradicted, they tried to overturn the infinite.

My concern about behavioral science today stems not only from its historical antecedents but from its methodology. Because it deals best with small, tightly controlled situations, it almost systematically ignores larger, often crucial consequences. For example, much medical and sociological literature concerning human behavior completely excludes discussions of ordinary, life-filling intimacy and its manifestations. My review of the indices of several widely used texts on human sexual behavior failed to show topic headings for *love, marriage,* or *children.* Another researcher reviewed over 500,000 references in the *Index Medicus* for 1970-1973. Only fifteen articles referred to love, and then only in relation to mental illness.[22]

In an effort to avoid complexities in research, many who specialize in human behavior ignore powerful, profound, universal realities of which steady, sturdy homemakers—both fathers and mothers—know a great deal. Love, marriage, and children are the themes of their existence. To dismiss as irrelevant these admittedly complex yet universal phenomena in favor of the fragments studied in formal research is at best irresponsible and at worst intellectual arrogance. The consequence is deadly for human intimacy.

Consider, for example, this fragmented approach to love and commitment:

> Jack and Ed have . . . entered into a relationship by which they are beginning the same pattern as a heterosexual marriage. They will accumulate, they will buy, they will sell, they will rear and visit children by former marriages, they ultimately will hope to live comfortably in retirement on the estate they have garnered during their life together. . . . Jack, thirty-seven, who owns his own business, and Ed, twenty-six, a corporate employee, have shared an apartment for about a year. They acknowledged that their relationship might be permanent, but further acknowledged that their friendship, *like any friendship,* could be terminated.[23] (Italics added.)

This fashionable equation of homosexual liaison with heterosexual marriage is sophistry and contains its own fatal inconsistency. A relationship that can "be terminated" just "like any friendship" is not very satisfactory even as a definition of friendship. It certainly has no legal and cultural standing as a definition of marriage. Marriage is formal, exclusive, and intended to endure. Friendliness within marriage is a blessing, but friendship is a pallid description of the profound intimacy which is implied by marriage. An association that all along assumes its own termination cannot logically be the same kind of relationship as that which assumes its own continuation—and continuation is an element inherent in marriage.

In a widely advertised ten-year study of homosexuality, the authors concluded that homosexuality was a positive way of life because, among other things, the homosexuals they studied were more "exuberant" and had a larger number of friends than heterosexuals.[24] The temporary and fragile relationships of the ironically nicknamed gay subculture—most of them promiscuous—and the euphoria which characterizes many in it—all too often accompanied by a matching depression—were interpreted as superior to the more disciplined, orderly lives of the heterosexual subjects.

As another example of the unreliability of some professionals, a prominent behavioral scientist recently urged in a public debate that suicide not be interfered with since, he asserted, suicide is a personal, civil right. A questioner asked about the effect upon family members. The response was that such concerns are "irrational" and "unscientific." Yet, in reality, family members are shatteringly affected, if they are emotionally normal. One wife's case, reported in a popular national magazine, may be typical. She considers the suicide of her husband with painful emotion: "Dick's suicide casts a horrible shadow on those who knew and loved him. The shock and sorrow were, and are, insurmountable. . . . Why couldn't I have saved him? He had been the best friend I ever had. I must not have been a good enough friend to him. I wanted to piece it together; I relived every conversation. But there were no answers, and it didn't fit together."[25] This agony is far removed from a passionless discussion of "rights."

However, the presumption of science in challenging universal, time-tested values and standards of conduct has not gone unremarked. Donald T. Campbell, as president of the American Psychological Association, called this trend into question and chided his colleagues for illogically ignoring the impressive weight of values based on tradition:

> I would recommend that as an initial approach we assume an underlying wisdom in the recipes for living which tradition has supplied us with. I also recommend that we use this perspective to edit our teaching materials in those areas where they conflict with traditional dogmas, removing any arrogant scientistic certainty that psychology's current beliefs are the final truth on these matters, emphasizing our need for modesty on topics on which we can do no experiments, broadening our narrowly individualistic focus to include social system functioning, and expressing a scientifically grounded respect for the wisdom that well-winnowed traditions may contain about how life should be lived.[26]

It is hardly a secret that much social science ideology has been formed in reaction against our traditional Judeo-Christian heritage. However, what began as objections to political-theocratic excesses of an intolerant state church has come to include rejection of religious moral values. A legitimate dissatisfaction with how fallible humans might have interpreted religion—or even with corrupt and corrupting religious institutions—should not make reasonable people throw out the pure principles at the foundation of that religion. In their injunctions to cherish human life, to accept and honor responsibilities, and to embrace values in oneself and others, these values are the foundations of our civilization and we will discard them at our peril.

Science as a tool is probably indispensable to our way of life. Science as a source of values is merely one voice among many.

Conclusion

There are genuine emotional risks in embracing the concepts that lead to intimacy. But if we base our lives upon illusions, we will savor neither the joys nor the sorrows of reality. Consequently, we will not learn from them and will thus risk remaining emotionally underdeveloped.

On the other hand, we should not imagine that reality is always trouble-free. Hoping that cruelty will disappear guarantees eventual despair, for it will remain. Wishing for beauty without creating it can lead to cynicism. It takes courage to invest in being alive, to reject illusory fragments, to refuse to deal with human relationships by the lowest common denominator, to accept freedom and our own responsibility for it.

Viktor Frankl, in *Man's Search For Meaning,* recorded his experience of spiritual intimacy while physically imprisoned in a Nazi concentration camp. He, with his fellow prisoners, struggled in the predawn winter cold toward their day's assignment as slave laborers. Despite abject misery, he understood and experienced a larger enduring reality:

> We stumbled on in the darkness, over big stones and through large puddles, along the one road leading from the camp. The accompanying guards kept shouting at us and driving us with the butts of their rifles. Anyone with very sore feet supported himself on his neighbor's arm. Hardly a word was spoken; the icy wind did not encourage talk. Hiding his mouth behind his upturned collar, the man marching next to me whispered suddenly: "If our wives could see us now! I do hope they are better off in their camps and don't know what is happening to us."
>
> That brought thoughts of my own wife to mind. And as we stumbled on for miles, slipping on icy spots, supporting each other time and again, dragging one another up and onward, nothing was said, but we both knew: each of us was thinking of his wife. Occasionally I looked at the sky, where the stars were fading and the pink light of the morning was beginning to spread behind a dark bank of clouds. But my mind clung to my wife's image, imagining it with an uncanny acuteness. I heard her answering me, saw her smile, her frank and encouraging look. Real or not, her look was then more luminous than the sun which was beginning to rise.
>
> A thought transfixed me: for the first time in my life I saw the truth as it is set into song by so many poets, proclaimed as the final wisdom by so many thinkers. The truth—that love is the ultimate and the highest goal to which men can aspire. Then I grasped the meaning of the greatest secret that human poetry and human thought and belief have to impart: *the salvation of man is through love and in love.* I understood how a man who has nothing left in this world still may know bliss, be it only for a brief mo-

ment, in the contemplation of his beloved. In a position of utter desolation, when man cannot express himself in positive action, when his only achievement may consist in enduring his sufferings in the right way—an honorable way—in such a position a man can, through loving contemplation of the image he carries of his beloved, achieve fulfillment. . . .

In front of me a man stumbled and those following him fell on top of him. The guard rushed over and used his whip on them all. Thus my thoughts were interrupted for a few minutes. But soon my soul found its way back from the prisoner's existence to another world, and I resumed talk with my loved one. . . .

"Stop!" We had arrived at our work site. Everybody rushed into the dark hut in the hope of getting a fairly decent tool. Each prisoner got a spade or a pickax.

"Can't you hurry up, you pigs?" Soon we had resumed the previous day's positions in the ditch. The frozen ground cracked under the point of the pickaxes, and the sparks flew. The men were silent, their brains numb.

My mind still clung to the image of my wife. A thought crossed my mind: I didn't even know if she were still alive. [She was dead.] I knew only one thing—which I have learned well by now: Love goes very far beyond the physical person of the beloved. It finds its deepest meaning in his spiritual being, his inner self. Whether or not he is actually present, whether or not he is still alive at all, ceases somehow to be of importance.

I did not know whether my wife was alive, and I had no means of finding out (during all my prison life there was no outgoing or incoming mail); but at that moment it ceased to matter. There was no need for me to know; nothing could touch the strength of my love, my thoughts, and the image of my beloved. Had I known then that my wife was dead, I think that I would still have given myself, undisturbed by that knowledge, to the contemplation of her image, and that my mental conversation with her would have been just as vivid and just as satisfying. "Set me like a seal upon thy heart, love is as strong as death."[27]

This man is not an emotional mystic. He is a psychiatrist, trained in a traditional skepticism of faith and transcendent experiences. Thus, when he published his account, it had significance beyond other accounts of concentration camp experiences and became one of the most widely read books of our generation. Myriads have responded to his witness of the transcendent reality of benevolent and intimate love. Barbaric treatment had purged him of illusion; and as a consequence, he discovered the reality of intimacy. Even though it was an emotional-mental experience, it was not an illusion, for he had known his wife and she had known him. In the reality of that intimacy, he transcended the hell of his imprisonment. He knew from experience the end from the beginning, distinguished the fragment from the whole. He knew intimacy.

CHAPTER TWO

The Reality of Identity

The ability to become intimate depends largely upon a healthy and complete sense of identity, which is critically affected by the quality of the parents' attention to the child. If the first relationship is happy and loving, it lays the foundation for future intimacy. If it is not, we can be crippled in our sense of self, our identity.

A second major contribution to the formation of identity comes when a child makes decisions and learns to predict the probable consequences of his actions. Parents play a vital role as their reactions to childish behavior teach the youngster which attitudes and behaviors are acceptable—indeed, whether he personally is acceptable.*

We also learn that a genuine respect for all the other "identities" around us is part of the lifelong development of intimate relationships.

We begin mortal life in the most intimate of circumstances, after the union of our parents' bodies and within our mother's body. At birth this primary intimacy is traumatically disrupted. As consciousness develops, we seek intimacy based on an expanding awareness of our identity as separate from but connected to our parents and other people.

As all parents know, their children have unique personalities from birth as if they had reached some point of personality development prior to birth which they brought with them as the seed of identity. This seed is the nucleus to which subsequent learning is attached. We *accumulate* an identity around that core.

* The masculine pronoun is used for convenience in such syntactic cases.

What we do in the first ten years of life strongly influences the next decade and so on until, in the fifth or sixth decade, if we have been fairly consistent, we resemble a grown-up version of the child we began as. A terrible childhood can be moderated or the benefits of a good one weakened, but, most of the time, what we learn at first leads to what we are able to learn thereafter.

Independent, yet dependent beings, we are immensely influenced by our initial life experiences with our parents. I believe this is one of those simple truths which we ignore at our social and emotional peril. The increase of disturbed families may be a trend of the times, but a trend is not the same thing as a step forward nor is there any evidence to suggest that the amount of suffering is diluted if more people are involved. The reality is that nurturing, benevolent parents are essential to their children's sense of identity and ability to achieve intimacy.

The benevolence or detriment of identity-building comes largely from how kind and encouraging in touch, word, and emotion a parent is or is not.

As the child learns to work, play, and eat, and attempts to perform countless other formative tasks, his identity is shaped by how his parents touch him, speak to him, encourage by a smile or discourage by a frown. Especially critical is how they handle his failures. First steps, first self-feedings, first efforts to make a bed, throw a ball, write a word, sing a tune—these can strengthen or weaken identity according to how, through touch or word or facial expression, a parent either encourages more efforts until the child achieves competence or discourages the child in his efforts until he views competence as unattainable.

By being touched harshly, the child learns to touch harshly. If he is touched tentatively, he learns that. If he is touched warmly, he also learns that lesson. These lessons, benevolent or detrimental, become the bases for intimacy in later years.

At one time I worked with a troubled man who was quite promiscuous sexually. Part of the origin of his troubles was revealed one evening when I attended his brother's wedding reception with him. His mother was greeting the guests by gestures and words of welcome, and most responded with a quick hug. Caught up in the mood, my friend reached to embrace his mother. She said the right words, she even put her arms out to him, but when he tried to kiss her cheek she abruptly pulled her head back. Her embrace became a push. Her son was crushed. I began to understand the weak identity which was at the root of his frantic search for physical intimacy.

In the formative first months and years of a child's life, parents have the power by touch, by word, and by other signals to strengthen or weaken his identity. Intimacy thereafter in adolescence and adulthood is largely a matter of learning and expressing touches, words, and affectional skills which convey our feelings to others. How each of us does this is unique, one's personal style. That we learn it is essential. That we need to learn it primarily from our parents is a crucial fact of life.

The Essential Parent

During the first eighteen months of life, we cannot meet a single condition for our own survival without help, always of the most intimate kind. For example, at birth we would starve if we were not fed. These demands gradually decrease until, by about age three, we are able to meet most of our minimal physical needs. Yet these technical skills are intertwined with our emotional needs. It is easier to learn to feed and dress ourselves, to control bladder and bowels, to strive and fail or strive and succeed, if our parents love us and show it. As they help us to master the tasks of living, our self-esteem is reinforced and a positive identity begins to emerge.

Much of what makes an environment friendly is its familiarity. A series of parent substitutes or a series of different facilities may disorient a child. Not only is he confused about them, but he is less able to define himself in relation to unfamiliar voices, mannerisms, aromas, and other stimuli. We see the same phenomenon at the other end of life when the elderly suffer dislocation, particularly if it is involuntary and involves separation from friends and supportive family members.

Intimate familiarity, with its enormous comfort, gives a secure base from which the child interprets the unfamiliar as something worth exploring rather than as a potential danger. The emotionally deprived child, on the other hand, attempts to consolidate his already restricted world into an even smaller and more controllable place. He either tightens his desperate grip on his few familiarities or he gives up all too easily. The secure child relinquishes, often with tears but without trauma. While all children initially are very self-centered, the secure child moves relatively easily to a larger world of things and relationships while the fear or passivity of the insecure child becomes the manipulative, uncompassionate approach to relationships of the selfish adults we have seen all too often in the "me decade." Because of this I anticipate a severely troubled generation of children in the 1980s and 1990s, compounding the problems of their parents into another unloving, unloved generation.

Many parents, their own identities vague, give little thought to their child until he is born and is an unavoidable reality; then they react rather than act and often have no coherent ideas about child raising at all.

Still other parents have clear philosophies based upon rational and considered ideas, but they may confuse control with intimacy as they try to coerce the child into total conformity with their standards and punish anything they perceive as disobedience, even if it is only spilling as the baby first attempts to feed himself. Thus they dictate an identity which the child may or may not accept.

In contrast is the benevolent reality of parents who have clearly distinct identities, who are bound together by deeply meant commitments, who desired to create this life through their emotional and physical union, who view themselves as "one flesh" and celebrate their mutual power to create and nuture their child. They also know and celebrate that child's separateness, guiding but not tyrannizing. This is not Pollyannish illusion but heroic reality. They intend to reward, discipline, accept, suggest, direct, give, take, listen, learn from and teach, suffer and exult with, and assist in providing all the realities of experience which their child needs to become a whole human being. These parents are flexible and respect the unique individual with whom they are entrusted—a welcome and cherished intimate, warts and all.

While no family can be expected to function flawlessly, there are those who do remarkably well. One such is the family of Doug and Carole. Both parents are strong personalities who expected their children to resemble them. Their two oldest children showed that they had inherited the strength, at least, by rebelling in an effort to develop their own identities. Eventually Doug and Carole understood that they were trying to impose themselves on their children, eased up, and encouraged individual expressions of personality, although they maintained firm values about character. After thirty-five years of experience, they have five adult children who feel free to pursue unique interests and express themselves individually, yet these children and their spouses share a strict set of moral values—even the two who experimented with rebellion. What Carole and Doug discovered was that each child is a separate and unique personality and that what parents can most effectively do is enjoy the child's personality on the one hand and work to add to that unique and perhaps nonnegotiable personality such character traits as honesty, kindness, diligence, self-esteem, and nurturance.

Dismissed by some as hopelessly idyllic, this type of family is not an illusion. Many parents and children experience this relationship, benevolent because it perceives and encourages good results. Through the ages husbands and wives have loved each other and the children they mutually create and nurture.

Out of their collective love have grown very stable—yet highly individualistic—identities. Parent substitutes, such as warm and skilled day-care attendants, without question improve on inadequate homes, but they are attempts to compensate for failure of the best approach, i.e., nurturant parenting in the home.

Burton White, director of the Preschool Project at Harvard University, discussing child care by people other than parents of intact, healthy families, stated:

> On balance, I would say that your own family is definitely likely to do a better job . . . than any day-care center you can put him [your child] in. The only place where you are likely to get a better set of early experiences for your child is in a family day-care operation run by a woman in her own home, provided that the woman has been one of the minority of people who has done an unusually good job with her own children. . . . Whether or not you find a superior home-run day-care operation is a matter of luck. The odds are against you.[1]

Parents, adoptive or natural, are essential in responding to the infant in intimate ways few others can or will. An adult, offered someone else's child to hold, notices unfamiliar smells, the sticky hands, and the runny nose. The nurturant parent matter-of-factly wipes the nose, cleans the hands, and cuddles the child. There are familiar games, little bedtime rituals, shared accomplishments—the first turn from front to back, the first sitting up, the first step, and the myriad unfoldings of identity which bind hearts. Erich Fromm describes this intimate process: "A child starts life with faith in goodness, love, justice. The infant has faith in his mother's breasts, in her readiness to cover him when he is cold, to comfort him when he is sick. This faith can be faith in father, mother, in a grandparent, or in any other person close to him; it can be expressed as faith in God. In many individuals this faith is shattered at an early age."[2]

The Powerful Infant

History, research, values, and unique human lives clearly demonstrate the surpassing importance of parental nurturance, especially in the first years of life; but the child is far from being a blank slate waiting passively to be written on.

Even though the human infant appears to be extremely weak and vulnerable compared to the young of animals, he is actually forming capacities which will eventually prevail over all other forms of life. From the moment of birth and probably before, his brain is incorporating, analyzing, and deciding. There is increasing evidence that even newborns make choices based on preferences. A baby repeats some behaviors and excludes others, seeks some sensations and avoids others, enjoys certain situations and dislikes others. He selects relationships by responding to some people and rejecting others. All of these acts demonstrate will and exert power. While a baby, by his mere existence, unintentionally influences his parents (do they resent him? pin all their hopes on him?), he also has the power to intentionally manage his parents.

A newborn begins to act, react, and apparently assess and decide. If the child is active, delighted parents respond to his body language and the child soon learns that he can initiate an embrace or play by his own actions. Lack of parental response or parents whose child may not be what they expect may create a situation where the child "learns" to initiate response by strident crying. The response may be harried and impatient—or, in terrible situations, abusive. And he learns to withdraw.

Thus, early on, the child acquires data about what works and what does not in creating a relationship. Actively loved, he grows in positive ways. Treated harshly, he fears and mistrusts. His power to get his needs met either enhances his sense of self or withers it. Either process influences his emerging identity as he begins to define how others will treat him.

The Predictable World

As a baby explores his world, he learns the import of word and sounds, touches and is touched, and stores data about causes and effects, especially in regard to his appetites and senses.

Clearly he cannot learn perfect predictability, because life is not that neatly ordered. What he learns is how to rehearse likely results and project likely consequences. The frequency of predictable results and consequences is his personal formula for security, identity, and, eventually, intimacy. In emotional terms, that two and two regularly add up to four rather than five or three is a major developmental discovery. He learns, for example, that even though his diaper is wet and cold, eventually it will be replaced by a dry, warm one.

This complex interplay of predictability was seen when our eight-year-old sustained an eye injury. As the youngest child he had received considerable attention from all of us. His role within the family was certain and secure, and we all enjoyed his pleasant personality. Because of an injury he underwent a long and delicate operation, wore an eye patch for months, then had a second and a third operation. He had to leave school for several months. His physical activity was restricted almost completely. He had to wear eyeglasses during all waking hours. There was pain, frequent medication in the eye, and distorted vision. This accident occurred only two months after we had moved from the only home, neighborhood, school, and church which he had known. Shorn of his security, he regressed rather sharply, needed seemingly unlimited cuddling, clung to his big brother, and imperiously gave orders from his bed. Almost every night he coaxed to sleep with us. Formerly adventurous, he now refused to leave the house, even with the family. It took long months before he regained his former security and confidence.

Under stress, when reality becomes unpredictable or unbearable, many adults resort to the gentler illusions of fantasy. We can only speculate about the internal life of a child living in emotional chaos; but apparently as soon as possible, the child also resorts to fantasy. One severely abused little girl rejected her human identity and became a dog in every possible way, because dogs, she had concluded, were petted and fed.[3] If reality is too painful, a child may learn that illusions are preferable to reality. But to choose illusions permanently locks him into a world which eventually imprisons his identity and inhibits intimacy.

This discussion does not mean that all fantasy is bad. Fantasy is a necessary part of the child's world, for it helps him build generalized images of people and their behavior as a background for his own predictable identity. Psychologist Bruno Bettelheim has shown how certain fairy tales, unlike television "kiddie" shows, deal with profound, universal themes. Fairy tales, games, and imagination are actually rooted in reality and show an inexorable, relentless groping toward intimacy, a process of sorting and ambiguity, establishing predictability, and defining identity. Bettelheim comments: "Ambiguities must wait until a relatively firm personality has been established on the basis of positive identifications. Then the child has a basis for understanding that there are great differences between people, and that therefore one has to make choices about who one wants to be. This basic decision, on which all later personality development will build, is facilitated by the polarizations of the fairy tale."[4]

Some children learn to accept unspeakable brutalities as a normal part of daily living. Others endure equally unspeakable emotional deprivation, more acceptable to society only because it is less obvious. It is our century's shame that we possess carefully documented accounts of healthy adults in concentration camps who chose to die when life no longer held any emotional satisfaction. We have no reason to believe that children cannot make the same choice.

There is considerable evidence that a child's efforts to define himself depend on whether he finds his world personally rewarding. If it is, he learns to share, give, wait, defer, and in other ways demonstrate his personal prediction that he will be fed, embraced, cleaned, and loved. If it is not, he becomes listless, dull, and apathetic. He withdraws from active exploration and improvement and ceases to seek or respond to loving gestures. A fortunate few fight back, noisily demanding attention and feeling rewarded when they are punished for being annoying.

There are a few exceptions who, in spite of the odds, overcome and excel. But sadly, these "invulnerable" children prove rather than disprove the rule as they unexpectedly survive traumatic childhoods.[5]

The subject of infant sexuality is also important in understanding how a child perceives the world. Many follow Freud in believing that young children are sexually active and that repression of these sexual instincts or urges damages the identity. In contrast, certain more recent authoritative books about early childhood, such as Burton White's *The First Three Years of Life,* do not deem childhood sexuality important enough to emphasize.

Childhood enjoyment of one's own body should not be confused with mature sexual experimentation. A therapist can usually predict difficulties in families when parents react harshly to childish genital curiosity and self-manipulation. To condemn self-discovery teaches the child that there is something wrong about intimacy with self, with touching and enjoying one's own body. Appreciation of one's body is a most strengthening and benevolent attitude, while rejection is a serious detriment. It is almost impossible for a child to dislike the body and its processes while at the same time trying to establish a positive sense of identity and self-esteem.

Even within the womb our bodies are neurologically capable of responding with pleasure to enjoyable sensations of sound or touch. Tactile pleasure is an essential part of identity. It is an immediate, reliable, therefore predictable, and pleasant reality. To be taught that it is evil or unnatural seems itself evil and unnatural.

However, to assume that childhood tactile pleasures are somewhat like adult sexuality is simply not justified. The extreme extension of this idea is the terrible exploitation of children in kiddie-porn or incest, especially the proposal by some that "legitimate incest" is actually beneficial to children. Essayist Benjamin De Mott attacks that proposal with barely contained anger:

> One or two truisms about parental love and children's needs perhaps bear restating here, despite their familiarity. To be loved for oneself, for what one is rather than for what one can give or become, is for a child as urgent a longing as that for physical nourishment. But few children can know from infancy the difference between being loved for oneself and being used. Few can easily distinguish the love that seeks nothing save happiness in the child's happiness from that other inner condition that, masked as tenderness, can contemplate persuading a child, against his or her good, to serve an elder's sexual appetite.[6]

Learning Fidelity

Infants and children cannot roam from intimacy to intimacy but attach themselves strongly to a small number of people with whom they feel secure enough to be fully intimate. The right combination of smells, sounds, and sights stimulates and reassures a child physically and emotionally. The wrong combination triggers resistance—even flight and severe anxiety. Some might call this dependence or conditioned response. However, such an interpretation fails to account for the consequences of predictable but unemotional care. Retarded people, as an example, will ignore almost any creature comfort in favor of an embrace and refuse to deal with an unkind attendant. It was as an attendant serving in such an institution that I began to glimpse the need for faithful, loving relationships.

In childhood, adolescence, and old age, humans seek a few close relationships. Those who try to substitute numbers of encounters for depth of commitment are usually disappointed. Intimacy cannot exist without fidelity, and fidelity is learned when children form predictable attachments that nourish their sense of identity and self-esteem.

Learning Self-Esteem

The two counterfeits of self-esteem are raw, ungoverned obsession with self and a total disregard for self that masks self-contempt. Self-esteem lies between, in a healthy and respectful relationship with oneself and with others.

The openness of American society is a monument to individual rights, but it is easy to cross the line from self-esteem into self-indulgence. Both excessive indulgence and excessive deprivation in childhood lead to self-focus in adulthood, a common problem in our society today. Excessive anything—playing, crying, eating, sleeping, being corrected, being held—has costs that the child learns to predict. Instead of indulgence or deprivation, we need opportunities to reward ourselves while accounting for the needs of others. Those opportunities will enhance the development of a healthy sense of identity, for intimacy grows as we learn to share and interact, whether on the school playground or at the family dinner table. Our self mingles with other selves, vastly increasing the potential for enjoyment as the concept of *us* unfolds. A toddler enjoying control over his own toys learns a different enjoyment from sharing his toys, having playmates share theirs, and playing cooperatively.

This process of one self discovering other selves is worth any parent's time in a simple research project. Go to a place where children are required to interact, such as the school playground or the backyard, and where you can observe without being seen. Select two or three children and watch them for fifteen minutes. Make mental or written note of character traits such as sharing, retaining, helping, cooperative play, isolated play, passivity and aggression. Then observe another set and perhaps a third. Having gathered this information about other people's children, then do the same research about your own, observing at different times of the day and different days of the week to account for after-school tension, hunger, weariness, and so forth. From these observations, parents can determine reasonably well what relationship skills their children need help with and which ones merit reinforcement.

A healthy sense of self can be perverted into self-focus if children are not taught sympathy and cooperation. The self-focused person actually excludes all the other selves in the world. The self-rejecting child who gives up all his toys or is desperate for his playmates' approval likewise becomes a troubled and one-dimensional adult. Intimacy derives from esteem of self that has been tried, tested, and refined, and has been rewarded by the expectations and reactions of other people in our world.

An example of the problems of unhealthy self-image is the case of Anna, a competent and vigorous woman who was always helping neighbors and relatives. In fact, people were afraid to decline her attentions because they sensed she would be hurt, even though her own home and three children were neglected. Eventually, overcommitted, she became ill. Her illness spiraled into deep depression when she could no longer make busy helpfulness her identity. Ironically, she began to recover her energy and direction when she accepted her own needs and interests as normal and necessary. As a child, she had learned to please her parents at all costs; and to her, identity was what others said it was or ought to be, rather than an inner sense.

Ila, by contrast, helped everyone too, but her assistance sometimes took the form of pointing out when others were being selfish or doing mediocre work. She was known both for her very high standards of performance and her willingness to go the extra mile to help others. It was also well known that she did not appreciate interruptions while she was working on her own projects. Anna tried to find identity by pleasing everyone. Ila had identity enough to share liberally yet withdraw into private activities which refreshed her. Her own identity was a source of strength and pleasure to her.

Conclusion

Identity is somewhat like a chameleon; the surface may change shades depending on the situation but the creature itself must be solid. If secure, we enhance the identity of others. If insecure, we undermine other's identities. By our relationships we strengthen or weaken, inspire or discourage, approve or condemn. If benevolent parents have reinforced our childhood formation of identity, we build upon that foundation. If not, we seek and search further, weakened usually from emotional starvation. To survive, we adopt the sterile contacts of "yours-mine." We lose self-esteem and replace it with self-focus.

Intimacy includes our ability to enhance other identities and to be enhanced. Without this, relationships drain and exploit because there is no intimacy, only mutual anxiety and loneliness. It adds to our happiness if we are valued by ourselves and others for what we are. If we are valued for how we can be used to gratify someone else's needs or expectations, then we are hampered in our ability to establish intimate relationships.

In *The First Three Years of Life,* Burton White of Harvard University concludes:

> I have devoted my whole professional career to pursuing the question of how competent people get that way. On the basis of years of research, I am totally convinced that the first priority with respect to helping each child to reach his maximum level of competence is to do the best possible job in structuring his experience and opportunities during the first three years of life. Now, if I am totally convinced of that concept then it becomes painfully obvious that to me, at least, any other kind of job, be it formal or informal, working as an engineer somewhere, working as the president of a bank, working as a career professional in designing, or in the arts, cannot really compete (in humanistic terms) with the job of helping a child make the most of his potential for a rich life. Therefore I do not think any job is more important in humanistic terms than the one this book describes.[7]

In short, the ability to love in whole-hearted intimacy as an adult begins in the experience of having been loved as a child. In an environment of warm and familiar predictability, surrounded by people who celebrate his individuality without suppressing their own, a child begins to develop a strong sense of identity. Thus fortified, he can move on to the next major prerequisite to intimacy—acquiring roles through which he can express his identity.

CHAPTER THREE

The Illusion of Stereotypes The Reality of Roles

Roles help make us predictable to ourselves and others, allowing others to begin understanding us, especially in regard to our maleness or femaleness—our gender. If we do not have a clarity and comfortableness about how we live our roles, we may have trouble developing intimacy.

Roles are flexible and are largely determined by our culture. We learn many roles (father, wife, church member, employee, citizen, student, etc.) but sometimes we are expected to learn roles which conflict with our identities. This is seriously detrimental to intimacy.

Gender roles—male and female behavior based on biology—are far more flexible than has often been assumed, but reality reminds us that some behaviors are gender-related. The biological differences are obvious. Less obvious, more flexible, and equally important are social roles drawn from those biological roles. Understood and honored, these roles enhance intimacy by their benevolent and remarkable complementarity. Misunderstood, those roles can create great pain.

Stereotypes about gender roles have long interfered with identity and therefore intimacy. Who could estimate the number of relationships that have been damaged because "women are so indecisive" and "real men never cry"? Especially troublesome have been the stereotypes of male superiority and female inferiority. The demolition of this stereotype is both overdue and welcome, but its replacement by a female stereotype which imitates this discredited male one is ironic and distressing.

To achieve intimacy with self and others, we must define roles for ourselves which are free of illusions and which harmonize both with our real, innermost identity and with the identities and realities of other people.

Developing Roles

Even though identity is the bedrock of our personalities, it is not enough. It is necessary also that each of us present a public version of his inner identity. This public self is our role, tied to gender and designed to make us predictable and understandable to others. This secondary self, or public role, is based mainly upon what society—family, friends, teachers—expect us to be; for example, student, athlete, and musician. Part of that role is gender based and includes the habits, grooming, dress, speech, manners, games, and relationships which are considered appropriate or normal for a boy or a girl, a man or a woman. It is to this concept that some strenuously object—and with some justification, as women in particular have been denied expression of their identities in some aspects. The dangers are real of allowing a role to become our identity, to role-play relationships rather than develop relationships based on our inner realities, and to become so excessively aware of society's expectations that we either follow every change in role slavishly or are caught off-guard and feel betrayed when society no longer reinforces a role. For instance, the recent emphasis on involved fathering tells many a middle-aged father who formerly concentrated on earning an ever-increasing income for the family that he has been a "bad" father for not spending more time with his children. If that father has assumed the role of wage-earner—and luxury-earner—primarily to meet societal expectations, then we can understand his anger when he is reproached for succeeding at it.

The danger is particularly acute if the role one derives one's identity from is a gender-based stereotype; for instance, the materialistic and sexually opportunistic macho male, the "cute" but helpless female. In American society, it is unusual for men to embrace each other. In Latin societies it is acceptable for men to embrace each other. The constraint on an American male, whatever his inner identity, is one of role.

To some extent, all of us must surmount the limitations of role. For example, close association with one well-known man over several years revealed to me a version of the male leader role quite different from the stereotype; the consequences of his behavior are more significant than his name, title, or affiliation. At first, as a businessman and lay religious leader, he was not particularly demonstrative, even though he gave considerable time to the troubled people he sandwiched into a very busy schedule and would, in fact, delay meetings on important financial matters to spend time counseling a troubled husband and wife. He had a keen mind, physical and emotional strength, and the ability to deal incisively with problems. As time passed, he seemed ever warmer until he was responding to people as if their nurturance was his whole motivation, in large groups or with single individuals.

After one meeting, he greeted several hundred adults and children as they filed out. Each received a brief handshake, a quiet word. For months after, the members of that congregation recounted special emotions about the momentary intimacy they had shared with this man.

On another occasion, in the evening before a long foreign tour, he telephoned to inquire about the well-being of a man in whom we were both trying to help change some very destructive behavior. With literally world-wide responsibilities, this leader's mind and heart focused on one lonely person.

In his later years, he became very expressive. He held the hand of the man or woman he was talking with, frequently greeted or bade farewell with a kiss on the cheek, a gentle embrace, or even a lingering hug. Frankly, such physically expressed affection was uncomfortable for me at first until I realized that powerful cultural role limitations were preventing me from accepting the simple truth that this leader loved people and delighted in expressing it.

From the time of this realization on, rigidly defined male role behavior has concerned me. I see everyday many examples of men unable or unwilling to nurture while behaving in role-defined insensitive ways which are acceptable and even applauded. The father demands that his young son practice soccer until the boy has tears of weariness and embarrassment in his eyes. They leave the field separately as strangers. Another father seated in church sternly rebukes his three-year-old son for trying to hug him, all the while cuddling his daughter in his lap. A financially strapped man earnestly asks advice from a colleague and the colleague, embarrassed by a serious conversation, makes it clear that friendly banter is the only level of conversation he will accept. A neighbor recuperating from a serious accident rejects visitors because he cannot handle their sympathy.

For me, learning from that affectionate older leader how men can actually care for themselves and for others has challenged most cultural definitions of maleness which I find in popular and professional literature and has helped me to see that there *are* many nurturant men who are overshadowed by noisier, more obvious, macho types. I feel great reservations about letting my children—both boys and girls—absorb ideas about maleness from television, including Saturday morning cartoons. Of course they are caricatures, but the qualities caricatured are pathetic inhibition and machismo.

Professional literature also abounds with such distortions, the most striking being the obsession of some sex therapists with restoring erotic functioning rather than restoring nurturance. Almost all measures of such cures involve a certain quantity of acts rather than a certain quality of relationship.

If there is a "most wanted" villain whose crimes account for the greatest loss of intimacy among us, I nominate that role expectation which denies men, and their wives and children, the expression of tenderness.

A dramatic example is a gang subculture where, as one influential pioneering study indicates, fragments of personalities meet, mate, and abuse themselves and each other. These are with partial identities derived from a single role. Through their fragmented groupings they acquire, as a group, a pseudo-identity which is immediately lost if they go outside the group.[1]

I saw the same phenomenon often in juvenile court. Young people who committed aggressive crimes in groups, often under the influence of drugs or alcohol, would, alone with a counselor, be confused and passive. Frequently, the most effective therapy involved constructing a role and identity which did not depend upon peer reinforcement. In reality, these so-called rebels were desperate conformists.

Furthermore, history itself teaches us of the immense flexibility of roles. As only one example, a teacher must today know more than the student, attend class daily, and examine the student's knowledge. However, during the medieval emergence of the university, students hired and fired their teachers and contracted with them to teach the subjects the students wanted to learn on a schedule acceptable to the students.

But flexibility is not equivalent to dispensability. It is one thing to redefine *teacher* and quite another to dispense with *teaching*. It is exhilarating to contemplate the many ways an individual may choose to be a man or a woman but rather chilling to listen to proposals that would eliminate consideration of gender in all cases. It seems far more profitable to enjoy women's athletics and men's athletics equally than to worry about artificially integrating teams, for example.

The importance of harmony between gender and identity has been underscored by the recent decision of the Johns Hopkins Medical Center to discontinue sex reassignment operations. Soon after the operations, researchers found their operated patients were actually "slightly more distressed" than the unoperated group. In further follow-up two to five years later, even though both groups "reached comparable adjustment levels," this slight difference increased until "the degree of positive change approach[ed] significance" for those who had the operation but was "clearly significant for the unoperated." The report concludes: "Those patients who pursued surgery, particularly those who pursued it precipitously, showed levels of distress closer to initial levels."[2] In other words, the operation simply didn't help very much.

The ideal of role development is to harmonize the private self and the public self. As we know ourselves better and achieve intimacy with ourselves, we increase our ability to relate to others as predictable, reasonably consistent individuals. If our identity and our role conflict, however, others literally cannot "get hold" of us.

Because role is a vast sociological topic, in our consideration of roles and intimacy we shall discuss only three aspects: gender stereotypes, procreational roles, and sexism.

Gender Stereotypes

Given the reality of gender, we can attempt to deal with it in one of three ways: we can discover what society dictates as appropriate for our role and surrender to that controlling image, we can deny that gender has any importance, or we can harmonize our individual identity with those portions of a gender-based role we find comfortable and appropriate.

I feel that the most hopeful route for human development lies in the third option—accepting gender-based differences and developing our own personal roles from them. It has been my observation that there are gender-based differences that affect roles, differences that have defined family responsibilities for thousands of years in healthy, clear ways. It has also been my observation that these differences are fewer than some suppose and, when they become rigid and narrow, they cause harm. Christian philosopher C. S. Lewis, who married in his middle years and lost his wife within a few years, eloquently deplored the prevalence of distorting stereotypes.

> For we [he and his wife] did learn and achieve something. There is, hidden or flaunted, a sword between the sexes till an entire marriage reconciles them. It is arrogance in us to call frankness, fairness, and chivalry "masculine" when we see them in a

> woman; it is arrogance in them, to describe a man's sensitiveness or tact or tenderness as "feminine." But also what poor, warped fragments of humanity most mere men and mere women must be to make the implications of that arrogrance plausible. Marriage heals this. Jointly the two become fully human. "In the image of God created He *them*." Thus, by a paradox, this carnival of sexuality leads us out beyond our sexes.[3]

Both sexes are either tyrannized or abandoned by society through unreasonable stereotypic definitions of gender-role behavior. No man with whom I have had thoughtful, probing discussions consciously aspires and works toward the macho image of toughness, aggression, and lust, yet if this stereotype did not offer a significant self-image to a significant majority of American adults, every beer commercial on television would be cancelled. If you are male, as a child you were probably discouraged from playing with dolls; tears were not what "brave" boys shed; and rough-and-tumble games were the rites of passage to peer acceptance. If you are female, as a child you seldom were captain of the team, you were guided into non-science classes, and you learned early how to beguile boys.

The stereotypes of male and female roles are deeply rooted in our culture. Bem's interesting 1974 gender role inventory[4] categorizes certain personality traits as masculine, feminine, or neutral. Some of them are:

Masculine Items	Feminine Items	Neutral Items
Acts as a leader	Affectionate	Adaptable
Aggressive	Childlike	Conscientious
Athletic	Compassionate	Conventional
Competitive	Does not use harsh language	Happy
Defends own beliefs	Gentle	Inefficient
Dominant	Loves children	Likable
Forceful	Loyal	Reliable

Independent	Soft-spoken	Sincere
Makes decisions easily	Sympathetic	Solemn
Self-reliant	Tender	Tactful
Strong personality	Understanding	Truthful
Willing to take risks	Warm	Unpredictable

Believing ourselves to be egalitarian and modern, we tend to react to a list like this by insisting that of course men can be gentle and tender and that certainly women can be competitive and forceful. Yet if one of our male acquaintances actually pursues placid pastimes exclusively or is so tender that he weeps, we tend to question his *manhood.* If a woman speaks forcefully and is competitive, we often tend to view her as *mannish.* In this time of rapid social change, which makes flexibility and egalitarianism newly fashionable, and when nontraditional ideas become the new orthodoxy, there is always an ultraorthodoxy that advocates a new rigid position. The most conspicuous example may be the scorn heaped on the woman who chooses and enjoys traditional activities of child care and house care without other major professional or community commitments.

How intriguing it is, perhaps even profound, that all human embryos are basically alike, sexually undifferentiated, during the first quarter of development! Given this biological fact and given the need of humanity for benevolent intimacy, is it not more appealing to drop the desperate means and ends of *both* stereotypes—that men and women should be completely different or that men and women should be completely identical—in favor of being human beings first? Thus, men would be tender and nurturant, and women would be tender and nurturant—or whatever other traits *human beings* possess. In this human way, gender roles would derive from identity, rather than being imposed on identity. For all the noise and tumult about individualism today, many still miss the basic point: that people ought to be free to interpret roles as identity inclines them, but within the realities of biology and culture.

The fact that men have had—and misused—their power over women does not mean that women should wrest the power from men. This newer stereotype is only a slavish imitation of the older. Men and women do need to change. The goal is not power but intimacy. Yes, it is time for women to rejoice in their capabilities and to be respected as whole individuals. Yes, it is time for men to be liberated from the crushing expectations of intellectual superiority, greater sexual capacity, and absolute emotional control. The order of the universe is hardly affected if boys and girls wear their hair the same length, or if the husband is reading stories in the nursery while the wife is reconciling the family bank account. But the universe—or at least our tiny corner of it—may be quite seriously affected if we think we can repeal certain role expectations which have remained constant for millennia and which lie at the roots of human intimacy: procreation and nurturance.

Procreational-Nurturant Roles

Throughout history in all known cultures, gender roles have been based upon procreation and related responsibilities. The nature of these responsibilities and their relation to procreation and nurturance are flexible only within certain limits. Childhood games, fantasies, and aspirations have centered around growing up to be mothers and fathers. No known language is without these words, even though many of the tasks assigned to each will vary. And these distinctions are essential. Without them, we lose both the ends and means of identity and role. Try to describe adulthood without alluding to marriage or parenthood. You find yourself listing traits or appetites—*responsible, decent, hungry, sexual*—but you are hard pressed to describe an identity, a role, and a purpose.

Television's appetite-focused advertisements and programs exhaust themselves in avoiding the portrayal of mature husband-wife, parent-child roles. The reader may want to conduct a personal experiment. Compare the amount of time in minutes that television programming in one viewing evening portrays infidelity, discipline, play, sorrow, physical affection (without sexual overtones), mature marital sexuality, family activities at home contrasted to recreational activities away from home, and so forth. The actors in such typical and well-crafted programs as *MASH* portray antifamily, antiparental roles. Colonel Potter is the only responsible, faithfully married character; and he is white haired and obviously over the hill, while his colleagues are still young enough to have "fun." The actors in other typical programs resort to adolescent-appetite situations and behaviors as they play football in the prime of life, solve and perpetuate crimes, and stage elaborate sexual pursuits free of distracting responsibilities of children or parents.

Of course, an individual may choose to remain unmarried or through circumstances beyond his or her control may be unable to marry. A couple may choose to remain childless or, because of infertility, lack of adoption options, or other circumstances, remain childless. Unless such choices are motivated by physical or major mental health considerations, can choosing to remain unmarried and childless be a mature choice any more than bearing children without intending to nurture them is? Current attempts at dispensing with procreational-nurturant roles is both irresponsible and arrogant. Two social researchers, analyzing social-emotional trends, warned that our society's "mass escape for fear of responsibility of filial obligations can infuse all human relations with unbearable chaos."[5]

Gender-based roles drawn from procreative responsibilities give structure and purpose to individuals and therefore to society. Eliminating these roles undermines our identity and, consequently, undermines our possibility for intimacy. The roles of adult-husband-father and adult-wife-mother, though more flexible than have traditionally been supposed, are still negotiable only within limits. Only women conceive and give birth. A woman can—and many have—abandoned their infants, but usually the psychology of bonding is enhanced by the physiology of nurturing. A woman focused upon her maternal role has a patience with and interest in her child that is not easily replicable by anyone else who has not invested the same kind of attentiveness in a child. The fact that the same bonding can occur between adoptive parents and children is gratifying evidence of the power of intimacy, once given the appropriate channel of tender, attentive nurturance.

Alice Rossi, in discussing the special nature of gender-related behavior, points out that there are many women with ex-spouses but very few with ex-children.[6] I believe, however, that many men have not only ex-spouses but ex-children as well, a perhaps predictable consequence of assigning the mother nearly all of the cuddling, feeding, eye contact, and countless other sharings with resultant olfactory, tactile, and hormonal harmonies.

This is not to say that a father should be another mother. On the contrary, biologically unaffected by childbirth, he is uniquely able to provide a secure climate during the vulnerable post-partum period. Even in intact families, as Michael Lamb has shown, the father tends to move in and out of the child's world more than the mother if she is the daily caregiver.[7] The advantage to an infant of having an unhurried caregiver who is undistracted by worries about overall family security is obvious. Unfortunately, such ideals are more honored in the striving than in the achievement.

From primitive hunter-gatherer cultures to complex industrial societies, women and men have pursued different roles related to their procreative-nurturant genders, though women have more often been involved in food production than men have been in infant care. A notable example from our technological present is Melford Spiro's twenty-five-year study of the Israeli kibbutz. This careful study deserves a careful look. Few human experiences have been more rationally planned, scrupulously studied, and severely tested. In the crucible of desert and danger, kibbutz life has been purged of many of the illusions which still impede our society.

The original kibbutz settlers were avowedly committed to eliminating every traditional role, gender distinction, and element of traditional family living. Based on a strong feeling that traditional roles stifled identity and discriminated against women, most pioneer doctrines were designed to radically revolutionize the female role. Dresses and cosmetics were replaced by shorts and shirts; children played, ate, and slept in age-graded houses; infants were nursed by whichever women had sufficient milk; married women retained their maiden names and kibbutz memberships independently of their husbands. Marriage was minimized by eliminating the traditional marriage ceremony and such terms as *husband* or *wife.* Public displays of affection were avoided.

Over half a century later, in this particular kibbutz the second- and third-generation sabras have almost totally reversed these doctrines and practices. Among the implications for intimacy and role behavior are

—A 50 percent decline in divorce, and a public climate "actively opposed to divorce."

—Care and concern for the couple's own children, seeing them as important to personal fulfillment rather than as obstacles to emancipation.

—Increased birth rate to a typical three or four children, with five or six not unusual.

—Family sleeping within the same house.

—Adoption by woman of "feminine" clothing and grooming.

—Domestication of apartments, with emphasis on baking, cooking, and gracious hosting.

—The return of "my husband" and "my wife," traditional wedding celebrations, public display of affection, preference for marital housing and privacy.[8]

As if to confirm the desirability of this virtual revolution, the pioneer generation seems to rather enjoy the changes made by their "apostate" children and grandchildren. Spiro records the delightful experience of a grandmother, who in her pioneering days had supported nonfamily dormitory rooms and other anti-traditional arrangements. Now, tending her grandson overnight, she reports that "she [did] not sleep the entire night, . . . thinking how 'thrilling' it would be the next morning to awaken and find her grandson with her. This woman was an intellectual and a strong feminist."[9]

Whether or not Spiro's Kibbutz Kiryat Yedidim is representative of other kibbutz experiences, it does not mean that all role behavior will invariably fit traditional role patterns. However, as Spiro's work suggests, there are both emotional and practical reasons why people in diverse cultures throughout human history have developed roles which are based on biological gender. This fact of history and anthropology merits respect by those of us who try to understand human behavior.

The procreative and nurturant roles of both sexes are under continual attack, with the media and those who have uncritically adopted its values regularly and not too subtly chipping away at the self-esteem of people who choose to concentrate their energies on parenting. Here are three not-unusual examples I have observed recently.

Example A: A news article about a woman appointed to a major federal position gave no family information, but noted: "She is, by every account, an extraordinary person—an outstanding judge on the ninth circuit court of appeals [sic] in California, a strong defender of civil liberties and, for good measure, an ardent backpacker who recently completed a 166-mile trek through the Himalayas."[10] To claim to cover "every account" but to omit marital or family history suggests that it is of no account.

Example B: A social scientist, featured for her efforts to become a "productive" person, said divorce from an encumbering husband was a necessary part of the process.[11] The message that productivity takes place best in the unmarried and public sphere is a disturbing one.

Example C: A university produced a series of fireside chats with impressive men, a list which included athletes, businessmen, and astronauts, but never a father per se.

In our time, working at parenthood seems almost unethical

—as though the father or mother were dodging more important social responsibilities. Full-time mothers are disparaged openly. So are men whose highest priority is home and family, not work or activities outside the family. A typical example is a friend in his forties who had achieved high status selling insurance. Taking stock of the family's needs, he and his wife decided to sell their large, expensive house, purchase a smaller one in the country, and make a career change to one that demanded less time and emotional energy. In effect, they determined to spend their money, time, and energy on their marriage and their children. Years later, they had achieved unusual marital and family success. Even so the man was criticized by some for "lacking ambition" and being "too domesticated."

Women are under the same pressure, as Dorothy Rogers's unkind comment indicates:

> The most traditional category of women includes the caretakers, those who marry early and have nothing else in mind but to pursue the domestic role. . . . In the past this option has been the most popular; women have simply lived for others and taken vicarious satisfaction in the achievement of their husbands and children. . . .
>
> Having become entrenched within the caretaker role, and without the desire, courage, or means to escape it, such women tend to rationalize their position by defending nonequal rights for women.[12]

No doubt some women are "caretakers" by default, not choice, but Rogers's indictment is extreme. At first glance, a friend and former client could fit this description of the traditional caretaker without the courage or desire to escape. Let's call her Gloria. In her late teens she married a man in his late twenties. They had three children in rapid succession. At first very dependent on her husband, she matured into a competent, confident mother who refused to continue the dominant-submissive pattern. This aggravated her husband, a talented, industrious, but insecure man. Anger and hostility filled their home as finances, friendships, and religion also became sources of conflict. "Yours-mine" negotiating offered only a temporary and deceptive haven, and they were discussing divorce when they eventually sought counseling. Counseling helped them transfer their energies from quarreling to communicating, since both had an interest in peace and harmony. Even though the counseling did not solve their problems immediately, it gave them some skills to use on the problems.

Over the next decade Gloria developed various talents to superior levels, earned income within the home, continued her intelligent and affectionate mothering, and worked on a redefined companionship with her husband. Today, a young grandmother, she is involved in her family, church, and community. She is assured, attractive, more committed than ever to the roles of wife and mother, soft-spoken, yet strong, and by "all accounts" an impressive human being in whom identity and role are richly complementary.

As Gloria changed, her husband developed an appreciation for her adulthood, helped her change from a child-bride to a companion and friend, and discovered that he liked her much better as an equal—and liked himself better, too. One of her married sons, well aware of past troubles, recently volunteered that the blossoming love of his parents for each other and their individual accomplishments gave inspiration and strength to all the children.

In certain ways these two people were stereotypically male and female. He was strong and silent, she emotional and dependent. However, as they both discovered, at first to their discomfort but then to their happiness, neither stereotype was accurate. Although reserved, he was deeply emotional. His silence came from suppressing very powerful feelings and needs. Gloria was actually quite independent. Thus two illusions had nearly added up to marital tragedy. After they recognized some basic truths, they began to nurture each other's true self. He was encouraged to drop the facade and express his emotions in a manner that was comfortable for him. She let herself enjoy her unusual talents, skills, and power of personality.

There is no doubt that Gloria had to make the greater effort initially. One of the primary factors which kept her focused was her unwavering desire to eventually enjoy her husband as much as she enjoyed her children. Her success—and her husband's—could not have happened if they had been untrue to themselves by allowing themselves to react or role-play to the other's stereotype. These two people, by their commitment to procreational-nurturant roles, are influencing the next several generations in their family. Together they are completing the larger experience of marriage.

The New Sexism

Although the differences between men and women we have discussed are real, there is also enormous complementarity of the two genders and roles which is often lost in the ugly warfare of sexism. The phrase "the opposite sex" is itself illusion, implying one sex (male) as standard and females as counterstandard in every way. I prefer the more accurate phrase, "the other sex," implying marvelously matched and reinforcing companions in life and applicable to either sex.

One of the most detrimental outgrowths of the "opposite sex" illusion has been the notion of female inferiority, often confused with the realities of social and biological role behaviors we have discussed. At the root of the "inferior female" myth is the fundamental and pervasive idea that male dominance is *the* model, instead of the political power issue it really is.

Some militant feminists, unaware of or ignoring the inconsistency, demonstrate behaviors which are not liberated female but rather are pathetic imitations of maleism. For example, one prominent activist began her first congressional day with crude language and arrogant egotism,[13] a display of stereotypic machismo. So long as the "opposite" sexes contend for power, intimacy must suffer. If one sex must surrender to the other, then power usurps intimacy. Seeking intimacy requires people to recognize and nurture the identity and the role of others as well as their own. It is illogical and harmful for those who decry the old sexism to propose that men should be increasingly free to harmonize their inner identities with their outer roles but that women should restrict themselves to the narrow stereotype the males are vacating.

It is ironic for women to exchange one tyranny for another, especially one which men would gladly surrender. History hardly endorses crude maleism as the avenue to intimacy. It is difficult to see how female chauvinism will produce more benevolent results.

Conclusion

Are the two sexes vastly and irreconcilably different? Is there really a war of the sexes? Hardly! Such ideas are part of the seemingly infinite list of illusions to which we have been subjected. Rather, our opportunity is to harmonize identity and role and expand both through companionate intimacy.

Constitutional male and female differences are determined by a few significant genetic factors—and these differences are very important—but there are not two *opposite* sexes; there are *not* superior and inferior genders. Accordingly, intimacy, be it social, emotional, or physical, is a means of achieving a more complete, expanded identity. Intimacy is further enhanced by the development of clear yet flexible roles because we then add to our private, unique self a public and predictable self. When people can deal comfortably with our public self, they can more easily enjoy shared, intimate experiences with us. It should go without saying, of course, that adopting a public role greatly different from our private self becomes crippling role-playing, not healthy role development.

Except for the major factor of procreation and several far less significant factors such as verbal and visual differences, large muscle vs. fine muscle control, etc., it seems that men and women can do many of the same tasks and adopt many of the same interests. Thus, women can be scientists and men can cook meals. But no man can be a wife and mother and no woman a husband and father. As Rekers put it, "We [must] distinguish between arbitrary sex-role stereotypes (which should not be taught) and appropriate sex-typing. There are specific behaviors that are inappropriate for males [or for females] under all circumstances."[14]

For centuries some men have sewn clothing, and some women have performed the heaviest manual labor. Women have empirically been proven to have naturally more nimble fingers, but many men have excelled at the violin. Women seem to be more gifted in verbal acquisition, but Daniel Webster and Winston Churchill were not women. Many traits know no gender boundaries. But every child so far has been born of woman and no child has been conceived without a father, even in a test tube. What can be the point in attempting to repeal the laws of reproduction and nurturance, those realities which give meaning to being male and being female? Much about woman's femininity is cultural as is much of a man's masculinity. But at present and for the foreseeable future, there are clear duties and opportunities which give special meaning to femininity or masculinity. Over thousands of years they have served mankind well in ordering all societies. Mothers have traditionally extended the security of the womb through the first several years of life, fathers have traditionally introduced the child to the world outside, and both have provided loving support and attentiveness to that child and to each other. To assume that these profound differences can be wiped away by intellectual temper tantrums is illusion epitomized, just as it is arrogance to assume that the two roles are unequal.

CHAPTER FOUR

The Illusion of Sexual Exploitation The Reality of Relationship Skills

Identity and role mean little unless we communicate and relate with other people. The intimate "games" people play with each other are often exploitive, and our urgent need for intimacy can render us vulnerable to illusions about relationships.

We all need to develop skills with which we can relate to each other. If our relationship skills are limited, so will be our relationships. Many people, rather than developing extensive social-emotional skills, seek the lowest common denominators of social and emotional contact—power, dependence, and sex, for instance. Usually the lowest common denominators are the quickest, least challenging means of establishing a relationship. They are almost always manipulative and exploitive whether exercised solo or in "yours-mine" contracts.

The task of learning to live together is a matter of learning how to relate our identity and role to the identities and roles of others, a lifelong task of acquiring a repertoire of skills—verbal, emotional, physical, social—to enhance our intimate relationships.

Despite a sense of identity and role, we need social-emotional and physical relationship skills. They are crucial to intimacy. Without them, we would be immobilized. Ideally these skills include not manipulative, aggressive "tricks," but thoughts, words, and touches which enhance self-esteem and convey respect and affection for others. These skills reinforce identity and role, adding rather than subtracting or maintaining the status quo. Small wonder, then, that skills of intimacy—not exploitation—lead to fulfilling intimate marriage, not "yours-mine" contract-making or downright promiscuity.

Often the difference between intimacy skills and sexual manipulation or exploitation is seen simply by how comfortable and respectful people are with their own and others' bodies. For example, as physical maturity becomes evident, emotionally immature young men and young women may resort to adolescent jokes about body parts instead of developing sensitive, kind appreciation of the human beings involved. The girl is hurt by teasing about her developing breasts; the boy is laughed at in the locker room if his body hair seems sparse. Ironically, the coarse language and crude humor become signs of "growing up" in teen culture while respect and sensitivity are jeered at.

For the person of social and emotional integrity, sexuality is a vehicle of expression, not a weapon or a game. Its innate excitement and pleasure give it value as an important part of life, but moving beyond mere sexuality to relationship skills of decency, modesty, empathy, and respect—a move which requires self-discipline, regard for others, and true integrity—also assures the intimacy of which sexual union is the crown.

Relationship Skills

The person who seeks to establish a whole relationship also needs to see the consequence of hasty, superficial contacts based on erotic experiments. Reality demands that he or she develop the social-emotional relationship skills which lead to trusting, enduring relationships. Because of Freud's influence, many see *all* male-female relationships, particularly in the teen years, as primarily sexual; and many adults, finding such precocity "cute," encourage behavior that is either implicitly or explicitly sexual.

The consequences of making this the overriding pattern in relationships from childhood on are simply that behavior outstrips emotional and social maturity, sometimes to the point that the child's too-hasty entry into sexual activity means that he never learns any other way of relating to others. He thinks of erotic contact as the goal of all human interactions, becomes narrowly skilled in such interactions, and bleakly wonders years later why he feels lonely.

When erotic behavior is the goal, potential relationships are limited mainly to those with similar goals, a demonstrably small portion of society. When people select relationships on such restricted bases as race or religion, they are denounced as bigots by those who know a wider and richer basis for friendship. Yet our culture has, ironically, glamorized the sexual adventurer as sophisticated when in reality he may be just another bigot, hiding from the complexity of full human relationships.

Two contrasting men come to mind here who both came for premarital counseling at the urging of their fiancées.

The first, Rick, was noticeably ill at ease, shifting in his chair, seldom looking at me, and speaking in a low, halting voice. He paid little attention to the young woman with him. His questions had to do with sexual behavior and little more.

Lyle, on the other hand, moved his chair so he could hold his fiancée's hand during the interview. He spoke clearly. His questions included finances and health as well as sexual behavior.

During the interview I found that Rick and his girl friend were already sexually involved and wanted to know how to increase their erotic gratification after marriage. Lyle and his girl friend had not engaged in sexual relations. They said they were eagerly looking forward to it but felt strongly about waiting until after marriage.

The impression I had of the two men was that Lyle saw his future wife as a whole human being while Rick saw his as a means of gratification. Subsequent experiences confirmed this observation. Rick imposed a stressful honeymoon upon his wife with his unending sexual experimentation. (Her feelings of being demeaned and exploited have been echoed by far too many other women whom I have heard discuss their honeymoons.) In contrast, Lyle and his wife enjoyed a honeymoon week in a secluded place where they became physically acquainted in an unhurried fashion, leaving their motel frequently to see local sights. They communicated in every way and their sexual relationship was a loving part of that communication, spontaneous and appreciative, with no element of "performance." In one case a marriage was begun. In the other, seeds of divorce were sown.

It is challenging and often difficult to learn the courtesies and the nuances which constitute relationship skills. Ours is an abrupt and hurried society. Not only does it take time to develop skills of basic courtesy and decency, it requires patience, discipline, and benevolent empathy for each other if we are to actually use these skills. We speed-read, exceed the speed limit, and eat "fast food." And we tend to initiate our relationships in the same manner. The result of fast, obsessive emotional involvements is a type of social-emotional hyperventilation, an obsession with sensual arousal based on the idea that the level of biological excitation two people can arouse in each other indicates the *quality* of an intimate experience. In fact, only fragments of personalities, not whole personalities, come together in this parody of an intimate experience. Tenderness, empathy, loving discipline, expectations, duty, and passionate fidelity are the roots—not the fruits—of committed intimate relationships.

Contrary to common belief, the new morality has produced shrinking pleasure, not the promised "liberation." One researcher who surveyed professional literature for several years, found almost no reference to kissing.[1] Another asked courting couples to engage in "contact comfort"—hand-holding, head on shoulder, arm around shoulder, etc.—excluding sexual thoughts or stimulation. It is a comment upon the fragmented quality of current relationships that these couples reported finding "contact comfort to be satisfying and thoroughly enjoyable,"[2] as if these gentle skills and emotions were new and promising discoveries.

Group intimacy is also a reality. World War II studies showed that soldiers, combatant or support personnel, performed better and had fewer emotional problems as part of an ongoing, close-knit group. Familiarity, tradition, and intimate relationships were critically important elements in their ability to cope with and survive the rigors and loneliness of war.[3] As might be expected, women in war situations expressed similar needs for intimacy but were more straightforward about their needs.[4]

Out of all the innumerable experiences of play, competition, and formal and informal education that prepare us for intimacy, none is more important than our family relationships, simply because of their duration. All other relationships are temporary. School is over, the party ends, the argument stops, and so on. But we never in childhood and seldom in adulthood "stop" the family. Within the family circle we learn attitudes, words, touches, competitions, cooperations, and emotions which are fundamental social-emotional skills. We practice at home, go outside and often fail, return home for coaching, and then go outside again. Often our practice sessions at home end in failure, but we are spared much of the pain because of the committed, attentive attitude of other family members. In our families, we learn to mesh with other people who have their own identities and roles. We learn to be social beings.

An excellent example of this process that I observed was an eight-year-old boy who was the despair of his parents. Bright and inquisitive, he tended, to put it mildly, to make his teachers uneasy. His curiosity about sexual matters prompted him to ask personal questions or make uninhibited comments which his teachers reported to his parents along with their fervent hope that such remarks would cease. The teachers were not prudes or rigid; they were simply reflecting the social understandings and mores that help us all live together comfortably. We do not stand too close, we touch only in certain situations, and we know how to suit our language and subjects to the occasion.

His parents sought my assistance in assessing his motives. Together we determined that he was simply curious, although a bit advanced, and explained clearly that some subjects were inappropriate to discuss outside the home. Rather than exhibiting shock, forbidding him to speak of such things, or harshly punishing him, as one offended adult demanded, they began to offer him a climate of discussion within their home. They responded openly but with discretion appropriate to his age and lack of experience. Disney nature films from the local library helped. Soon he was able to satisfy his curiosity at home and had also learned which words and subjects required a private setting. This process did not happen overnight; but after several months he had acquired important social sensitivity without a hampering sense of shame. His curiosity remained intact, the composure of his teachers returned, and he learned that words with sexual meaning were not ugly but special.

This learning process, so ordinary when proceeding benevolently inside an intact family, becomes more extraordinary when we see its lack. Among the severest of mental disturbances are antisocial thought processes and behaviors, often referred to as character disorders or sociopathic behavior. They include a marked lack of concern for, empathy with, or even awareness of the needs of others. People who are antisocial to this extent are not just rude, unpleasant, and grouchy. They are dangerous to themselves and others. They abuse their children, commit crimes, and damage the minds and bodies of friends, relatives, and strangers. They appear convincingly conventional and are frequently intelligent but use the skills of ordinary relationships to perpetrate extraordinary violations of common human decency. They usually have never experienced intimacy. They seem incapable of experiencing it. Anyone involved willingly with such a person is exploited; those unwillingly involved are victims.

This type of person is baffling to most people who almost always respond to right and wrong and affection and attention, have learned social skills, and hold social emotions, including guilt. One set of parents had to come to recognize this lack of conscience in a son. The more money and freedom they gave him, the more he demanded of them. He was never sorry for damages to property or hearts. Only after his parents adopted a strict punishment and reward program did he begin to control his behavior. Many penitentiary inmates show this same pattern.

If social skills are cut loose from the anchors of concern, compassion, service, fidelity, duty, and integrity, individuals can become antisocial. By this lack, the bonding agents of benevolent civilization are destroyed, as humanity becomes a mass of isolates who exploit each other to gratify personal appetites. Such self-focus becomes social malignancy. Like cancer cells, these individuals multiply their effects and infect others until the whole of society is diseased. Through this insidious process, evil becomes good and deviance normal, as an entire society falls ill. We must never forget that Hitler and Nazism were not abrupt and radical departures from the norm; rather they were the culmination of generations of the "sophisticated" German culture based upon the worship of power and intellect and contempt for the emotions, particularly those gentle and tender affections which tie people together through nurturance. Generations of such belief produced the barbarism of Nazi Germany where antisocial behavior became the norm and respect for the human body and spirit was swept aside by those who held no allegiance to universal standards of decency. It is not surprising that anti-Semitism and euthanasia evolved simultaneously with sexual chaos and sexually focused cruelty of the most bizarre type in that awful laboratory of the breakdown of individual and group intimacy.

A similar antisocial process can be seen in the evolution of certain modern sexual attitudes and beliefs which reject the wisdom of millennia of human moral values. What is one of the finest and most truly human pleasures has become, in many instances, approved pathological exploitation.

Childhood Sensuality vs. Adult Sexuality

Like other extremely detrimental distortions, sexual illusion can begin in relatively innocuous ways. Consider, for example, the concept of so-called childhood sexuality.

Freud's powerful mind cut through much foolishness of the Victorian era and attempted to sort out the components of childhood behavior which led to adult distress. Although many of his ideas are now out of favor, his emphasis on physiological behavior, from which he derived his famous oral, anal, phallic, latency, and genital stages, remains influential. Each stage is marked by sensory pleasure.

But there is a vast difference between the touching-caressing pleasures of the immature child, sensual interests expressed after puberty, and mature sexuality. The child's whole enjoyment at first involves simple sensory pleasures, including a warm body, a satisfied stomach, and cuddling from parents. As observed in chapter three, being deprived of these experiences damages the child's sense of identity. The young child, then, simply enjoys his own physical sensations and is not really aware of the tactile interests of his playmates.

Through the give-and-take of the playground, however, the child begins to learn rudimentary empathy and begins to realize that his behavior means something to someone else—a crucial discovery. Rapidly he moves beyond the sandbox to the more intricate world of the peer group, the school, and eventually society. He learns how to attract certain people and reject others, how to placate stronger children, and how to influence weaker ones, how to touch and be touched. The child learns and practices roles which enable him to become part of a group which reinforces identity and offers security. He learns how other people can either be enjoyed or used, enhanced or exploited. These childish and usually physical searchings of self and others should not be confused with desires for erotic episodes. Even Kinsey warned against this confusion.[5]

Later, during puberty when hormones increase, the capacity for sensory-tactile pleasure may increase. But more significantly, society's expectations change. Body changes such as growth of facial hair, deepening of voice, broadening of hips, development of breasts, etc., signal puberty to family, peers, and general society. They then begin to instruct the adolescent to direct his or her relationships toward paired-off sexual or pseudosexual activities. This cultural barrage is most unwise.

The physiological changes of puberty are profound but they are not radical personality changes. Personality has been unfolding from within the individual since birth. Long before adolescence people develop identity, role, and relationship skills. As Albert Bandura reported in his study of adolescents, there are not really notable changes in behavior at this phase of life.[6] For good or ill, teenagers continue to do what they have learned earlier, primarily from their parents.

The disservice, even damage, caused by accepting the dogmas of childhood sexuality and "explosive adolescence" is serious. It has often led to crippling distortions of identity and role. The healthy young child simply enjoys his body's senses in an ingenuous way, seeking relationships in the same way, but an eros-obsessed culture interprets these realities as the infantile version of adult carnality. When these same natural interests are expressed after puberty they are declared to be signs of mature sexuality. The tragedy of such an interpretation is that neither child nor adult can hold hands, embrace, sit cuddled next to someone, or kiss affectionately—male or female—without sexual overtones.

Sex Drive

Another dogma sees human beings as sexually driven and urges gratification of the "sex drive." This dogma has little basis in fact or even in logic. Lay persons and professionals alike use the term "sex drive" as if every one agreed upon its meanings.

Some of the confusion surrounding it is impressive in its imprecision.

One graduate-level college textbook teaches contradictions —wavering between statements about the powerful and involuntary sex drive and the demonstrated reality that sexual behavior is largely voluntary in humans: "Essentially, sexual problems are so prevalent because human sexuality *is . . . an intensely pleasurable and powerful drive which is irrepressible and constantly seeks gratification* and a response which is readily associated with painful effect, easily traumatized, impaired and distorted." (Italics added.) Then, later on the same page: "As previously discussed, sexuality is the most pleasurable of the drives. In contrast to the other drives which yielded pleasure primarily when they are quenched, sexuality yields pleasure even as sexual tension is building up. . . . *Sex can be delayed and diverted indefinitely and is highly malleable and infinitely variable in its expression.*"[7] (Italics added.) It is obviously confusing to be told that our sexual interests are simultaneously irrepressible and indefinitely divertable.

Definitions of the so-called sex drive range from a strictly biological necessity comparable to eating and breathing, to a predominantly social and emotional urge. One author defines drive as "arousal produced by physiological needs."[8] Another says drive is "genetically determined . . . [and] motivates the person into action."[9] The respected Abraham Maslow says: "The typical drive or need or desire is not and probably never will be related to a specific, isolated, localized somatic base. The typical desire is much more obviously a need of the whole person. . . . Indeed a stronger statement is possible, namely, that from a full knowledge of the need for love we can learn more about general human motivation (including the hunger drive) than we could from a thorough study of the hunger drive."[10]

Drive is a troublesome word because it interferes with efforts to understand why people enjoy one another by implying that we have no choice in those areas, that we are compelled. We are driven to eat and breathe by requirements of physiological survival, but our social-emotional efforts to eliminate loneliness, insecurity, and so forth are based upon social-emotional learning. Both types of efforts are powerful, but their origins and satisfactions are importantly different. We do not learn to have drives. We do learn to have needs and appetites.

As psychologist Kenneth B. Hardy points out, the alleged sex drive is actually an appetite learned from culture and reinforced by biology, its satisfaction institutionalized by culture.[11] Unlike true drives such as respiration or nourishment, this appetite can be, and often is, suspended for long periods of time with no negative effect. Its gratification is influenced by custom, values, and circumstances.

The crucial point is that there is not really such a thing as human sex drive which dictates that we *must* mate because genes or hormones order us to. In childhood and adolescence, we learn when, where, how, and with whom we shall be friends, playmates, and, sadly, enemies. In later years, we choose when, where, how, and with whom we shall be sexual. Childhood is a time when, if all goes well, we develop the capacity for intimacy. Puberty is the time when we develop the capacity for reproduction, a time ritualized by all known cultures in some form of "coming of age." But puberty is also a time when we can either learn to enjoy sexuality as a part of rewarding social and emotional experience or when we become addicted to sensuality as a major source of gratification.

Sexual-hormonal maturation introduces the potential for sharing or using our body in infinitely more powerful ways than before. Knowing that our sexual powers are voluntary, controllable, and subject to our values about intimacy is a very different concept than that like "other animals" we are biologically driven to mate. Analogies about human behavior from animal examples have gone far beyond reason in recent years, despite the protests of such well-informed critics as John Bancroft of Oxford University's psychiatry department that "there has been a tendency to extrapolate to humans from animal data in spite of increasing evidence of important species differences."[12] Zoologist S. L. Washburn ironically points out that musk oxen characteristically circle to defend themselves as did the British soldiers at Waterloo; should we infer that this was because of their genetic similarities to musk oxen?[13] His exaggeration makes the distinction between drive and choice.

The human body is a biological instrument by which we express nonbiological capacities. Satisfying survival drives keeps the body alive. Satisfying emotional needs and appetites through relationship skills is the uniquely human way we can embellish life. Intimacy is possible because of our total relationship skills, not as the result of a sex drive. Intimacy is a selective, learned, voluntary process, the outcome of developing compatible, shared passions of the heart, mind, and body. Its delights can be obscured by the illusion that we are swept inexorably and impersonally toward each other by biological demands.

Integrity vs. Lust

A remarkable example of sexual integrity is described by the brother of a retarded man—Roger—who married a retarded woman. According to the drive definition, sex would be just another natural urge to be gratified. Thus, these two should have been sexually active from the outset, especially since their retardation would prevent complex ethical scruples from developing. Instead, "with all their sexual knowledge and their declared love for each other, they had declined to participate in a full range of intimacy because they felt that was most properly done within the context of marriage."[14]

Assertions that sexual activity, rather than crowning and sealing the commitment of marriage, is "a process comparable to other natural functions such as respiratory, bowel or bladder function"[15] somehow tarnish even lust. That Masters and Johnson compare sex to such body functions confuses familiarity with intimacy. Though they condemn the old phobia that sex is dirty, they tie it to the elimination of waste. It contradicts clinical experience to extinguish the sex-dirt phobia by reinforcing the similarity. And though it is possible to argue that the relief that follows elimination is pleasurable in some sense, it is difficult to compare this individual and somewhat involuntary activity to the intimate nature of shared emotional passion or sexual pleasure.

If sex is a natural function to be performed when the urge strikes, then the complexities of human relationships are reduced to the simple problem of how to find a partner as rapidly as possible. Without question, we are naturally disposed to learn sexuality quite easily. We are also naturally disposed to learn speech, but few people accept uninhibited speech as desirable. What, then, would recommend uninhibited sexual expression as beneficial to mankind?

Like many other proponents of the natural function school, Masters and Johnson also sweepingly indict religion as a cause of considerable sexual neurosis. They decry "omnipresent religious orthodoxies" and bemoan that religion sees "sex as sin" and not simply a warm, pleasurable natural function.[16]

Masters and Johnson fail to distinguish between the religious encouragement of sexual expression within marriage, which the Bible clearly says is good (see Gen. 1:28, 31; 2:21-25), and religious condemnation of extra-marital sexual activity.

As I have counseled with sorrowing friends and clients after they have indulged in undisciplined sexual gratification, it has become increasingly clear that lust prevents and destroys intimacy. Lust, I have come to believe, is sexual selfishness. Lust seeks immediate gratification no matter what the other person feels or no matter what other obligations are violated. It is emotionally incongruent because it demands "love" through aggression. It is frequently illogical and distorted because it seeks pleasure by inflicting pain. Its consequences are detrimental to the self-esteem of both its victims and its perpetrators because it denies identity. Lust eroticizes fragments of people and fragments of relationships, always hungering, never satisfied. As one

Christian philosopher observed, "Lust is more abstract than logic: it seeks (hope triumphing over experience) for some purely sexual, hence purely imaginary, conjunction of an impossible maleness with an impossible femaleness."[17]

Should a person be unfortunate enough to wade through some of the world's scatological literature, among its many fantasies he or she would find numerous accounts realistic in their theme of lust-investing erotic episodes, exciting before consummation but afterward seen as ugly, sordid, even boring.

This was the reality of Dale's adultery. Over several months he saw in a woman at work everything his wife was not. He found his colleague intelligent, well dressed, and charming, while his wife seemed dull and slovenly. They committed adultery. The very next morning after the encounter, this heretofore glamorous woman suddenly seemed shockingly plain, even unattractive. In stunned reaction, he remembered his wife as attractive and pleasing and, with horror, realized he had violated his commitment to her. He was desperate to cancel his act of self-indulgence and kept repeating numbly that he couldn't believe he had done such a thing. His realization that he had suffered such a loss of integrity nearly destroyed him. What lust adorned with fascination, gratification revealed as illusion. I wish this were the only case I could give of such self-delusion, of such inability or unwillingness to assess consequences.

Our society romanticizes and merchandises the illusions of lust at all levels, from living room television to bizarre pornography. Most pornography is built upon aggressive lust, and one influential study found strong evidence linking pornography, aggression, and deterioration of sexual intimacy:

> We are not suggesting that "aggression is good for sex." Aggressive behavior that is stronger and more deviant than the mild, socially acceptable forms in our experiments, can interfere, we have learned, with the tender, affectionate feelings associated with sex. . . .
>
> We share the belief that the depiction of violence in erotica and pornography could be harmful.

> Psychologists, in our judgment, ought not to support, implicitly or explicitly, the use and dissemination of violent erotic materials. . . .
>
> We can foster those childhood experiences and human relationships that will diminish the attraction that the depiction of violent sex has for many people, and at the same time diminish the incidence of violent sex acts in our society.[18]

The illusion of lust is perpetuated by some popular fads in professional sex therapies based on the narrow theory that people are cured of relationship problems by acquiring sexual skills and having their erotic functioning restored. A careful scrutiny of these texts, especially the case studies, clearly shows that the crucial change factors are, instead, caring relationships and increased relationship skills.[19] For example, after Kaplan reports "Dora's" improvement during technical sex therapy (pleasuring exercises), she adds, "However, it is also important to note that Dora's new husband is kind and loving. . . ." Her first husband, with whom she received the same sex technique therapy, was not kind and loving, and they failed in therapy.[20] A crucial difference was obviously relationship, not just sexual proficiency.

Another example of the lust illusion is careless acceptance of masturbation as an inconsequential natural function. Fortunately, the idea that masturbation rots the brain, etc., has been exposed as myth, but new myths have sprung up. For example, a current myth claims that masturbation is both therapeutic and necessary.[21] Another myth, one of the more unfortunate, is calling normal infantile self-exploration and pleasure masturbation, as though it were sexually mature, intentional orgasm.[22] Kinsey's data have been misinterpreted to fuel an open, even aggressive, attitude toward masturbation. By lumping habitual, episodic, and infrequent masturbation together, the data collected by Kinsey and his associates have been used to conclude that almost all men and many women are involved *to the same extent.*[23] This incorrect interpretation has obscured a clear but seldom-quoted part of Kinsey's report, that with age and with maturity, masturbation "is the first major source of outlet [orgasm] to disappear from the histories" of the research subjects.[24] Further, Kinsey's data show masturbation decreasing dramatically for single males from a median frequency of less than about twice per week up to age fifteen to less than once a week by age twenty-six. For married males in the general population, the frequency is so small that Kinsey reports it as zero.[25] The probability is that habitual masturbation to orgasm is an unusual, even rare, behavior for men and women. Thus, habitual, obsessive masturbation results in a self-focused addiction that can be detrimental to intimacy. It is an emotional narcotic; like a drug-induced high, it creates a temporary escape but leaves the person depressed. Even pro-masturbation literature reports that masturbation "is often followed by an aftermath of disorientation, emotional let-down, and a sense of loneliness and separation from others."[26] Unable to obtain physical and emotional rewards in other ways, the habitual masturbator resorts to self-manipulation.

When masturbation is linked with fantasy, the individual can avoid testing himself against reality. Typically he imagines himself as powerful, controlling a fantasy partner. If such imaginary situations called forth responses of kindness, helpfulness, and sacrifice, they might serve some useful purpose. In fact, they often produce responses of imagined brutality, arrogance, and cruelty. Thus, McGuire and his colleagues found that traumatic episodes, reinforced by masturbation and fantasy, led to sexual deviance.[27] Some therapists have used masturbation and fantasy combined to substitute one type of aggression and exploitive behavior for another in their clients; shockingly, they term such clients "cured."[28]

Habitual masturbation, whether practiced alone or jointly in an emotionless but technically skilled mutual orgasm, is lust. It permits the person(s) to avoid the complexities and forces him to forego the rewards of intimate relationships. Allied with fantasy, it creates a world in which reality never requires an accounting. This is well known to publishers of such soft-core pornography as *Playboy* and similar magazines, long used as literal visual aids to masturbation. As a consequence the individual cannot develop the attitudes and behaviors which will help him develop and retain close and rewarding relationships. Masturbation's consequences are social-emotional isolation and erotic obsession. As two proponents of masturbation said—ironically, with approval—it "means that one need not please anyone else or take another person's needs into consideration."[29]

When no one else and no other circumstance such as personal values or self-esteem are considered, lust can become totally self-focused and impulsive. The ability to defer gratification of immediate appetites for later rewards is usually a hallmark of social and emotional maturity. It is no coincidence that impulsive, uncontrolled behavior of all kinds is one of the growing social and emotional problems of our time.[30]

Treatment methods employing masturbation and impulsive sexual gratification ignore the clear superiority of learning such potent relationship skills as simple kindness, courtesy, and empathy. And surely ethical questions are raised when a homosexual client receives electrode implants, masturbates to soft-core pornography, and is thereafter considered well because he then continues to compulsively masturbate and seduces a succession of women.[31]

Up to this point I have challenged several widely accepted ideas about sexual behavior. These ideas are so firmly entrenched in our society that subtlety will not serve my purpose. However, I would not want to uproot the illusion of the sex drive only to replace it with repression and denial of sex consciousness. On the contrary, those who perceive and welcome their sexuality as an important though not controlling part of their lives are uniquely prepared to make sexuality an honored aspect of building intimate relationships, one of life's richest and rewarding experiences.

Consider two people, Donald and Floyd. Floyd absorbed his culture's message about male relationship skills early—he learned to compete and win. He was not mean nor a bully but he did play every game, study every lesson, and date every girl to "win." Athletics were always contests, not games. Grades were reinforcements of ego, not measures of knowledge. Girls were indices of his social status, not unique individuals. Following this pattern, Floyd courted a woman who would be a career asset and whose pursuit was an interesting challenge. But instead of knowing how to enjoy her, he had to keep enjoying "victories." Their honeymoon and marriage were sexual and emotional contests. Floyd's relationship skills literally worked only in competition against an opponent. When his wife was cast continually as the opponent, Floyd won and she lost, until, in the end, they divorced. He had acquired skills which crushed intimacy.

Donald, like many other American men, acquired similar skills. But several years into his marriage he began to examine himself, his wife, Lorna, and what they did or did not have in their relationship. Many people who undertake such reevaluations fail because success requires assessing consequences accurately, throwing away deeply embedded perceptions, and acquiring new ones. It is usually easier to blame someone else for unhappiness. Donald was lucky. He was remorselessly honest as well as intelligent. In examining himself, he found that he dominated conversations, intimidated people, and was also impatient. Disliking these traits in others, he disliked them in himself and resolved to change. Secondly, he examined Lorna, not for her failings or even for her strengths but for her needs. He discovered that she had spent years of meeting others' needs without meeting some of her own. Her pain had accumulated inexorably. He also discovered that the degree of success in their marriage and family had come because she had made a conscious commitment to be a supportive wife, had developed the skills to build what companionship they did share, and provided nearly all of the nurturance their children received. Much of her success came in "working around" Donald, drawing him in when his cooperation was necessary, and excluding him when he interfered. Her own resentment at having to employ such tactics was part of the burden she carried.

Donald found it took practice and more practice to learn a new way of relating. He practiced keeping his mouth shut rather than criticizing. He practiced involvement in Lorna's preferred types of entertainment rather than his. He rescheduled his civic interests so she could have some. Then he discovered he was playing the martyr by pretending not to have any of his own needs met and had to rebalance things. Over time Donald learned new words, new moods to bring home after a hard day's work, and different methods of listening to Lorna.

Donald's changing allowed Lorna to change, but it took practice for her as well since she had largely learned to react to him over the years. Thus, both of them had to deal with habits of years' standing.

One of the severest tests came when she began to test his new-found benevolence by asserting her own interests and opinions. As she tested the pleasure of esteeming herself she came to expect to be honored by Donald. It was a kind of final revelation to Donald. He had been seeing himself as a heroic, enlightened male, nobly meeting Lorna's needs. This stance, he later realized, still put him in a "winner's" position. When Lorna demanded that he meet her as a whole person rather than as a collection of needs, he had to become a nurturant companion and friend. This was no simple transformation, but the bitter memories left behind from former behavior provided incentive. Fortunately, their commitment to each other was strong enough and the results from the changes Donald had already made were rewarding enough that he could let go of his last illusion of smothering dominance and really honor Lorna's identity, even subordinating himself on occasion. He later reported that it meant conscious practice for long enough that he could become automatically sensitive to others. It meant embracing and accepting an angry spouse or child rather than lashing back. It meant committing ahead of time and often without any guarantees of success to nurture Lorna in the very ways Donald was finally able to admit that he himself wanted to be nurtured.

He fulfilled his commitment in every way, from plodding, painful practice to exhilarating passion. Was there sexuality? Absolutely! But it became part of an ever-deepening relationship, enhanced by skills which built the people involved and the relationship they hungered to have—part of their relationship as whole people, not a substitute for it.

Conclusion

In human relationships the heart and mind do, in fact, rule. Satisfying the body's appetites is remarkably enjoyable, yet our intimate relationships are enhanced by kindness, empathy, and commitment, and are diminished by unkindness, self-focus and infidelity. Due to the data explosion about the human body, we have learned much about the biologic chemistry of intimacy but little about the psychologic and spiritual catalysts. To seek in biology the key to understanding relationships is to seek in vain. Alice Rossi, studying women in whom surgery had eliminated almost all androgens (the so-called libido or sex drive hormones), found their continuing sexual interest to be based on relationships, not lust or drive: "This is an important reminder that the affectionate component of sexuality is not physiologically dependent upon the erotic component,"[32] she noted.

Despite traditional wisdom and professional data which underscore the important of developing skills to build intimate relationships, much professional and popular literature persistently reduces human relationships to the low common denominator of appetite gratification through sexual exploitation. A detrimental consequence is to strangle enduring intimacies uniquely available to the human mind and spirit, leaving only a few limited and temporary lustful episodes.

Social behaviors based upon manipulation are alienating and detrimental. It is through sensitive response to others and esteem for ourselves that we live richly. By expanding relationship skills, we become more accurately sensitive to others. Attitudes and behaviors which weaken this shared empathy cannot be considered benevolent, for they harm our common humanity. Intelligent, warm affection for self and others is benevolent, good in itself, and especially good in its consequences. Rather than weakening, it strengthens identities and rewards role behaviors which enhance the social-emotional integrity of society. If we have built a foundation of identity, role, and relationship skills, we are prepared for the ultimate intimacy, marriage.

CHAPTER FIVE

Beginning Marriage: The Illusion of Cohabitation The Reality of Homebuilding

Marriage is the relationship toward which most of us direct our social and emotional interests. A good marriage brings ultimate intimacy through intense, united "homebuilding," and this is so despite the fact that some commentators view marriage, the family, and its traditional roles in general as threatening to identity and individual happiness. Cohabitation means merely living together without investing in the relationship and can apply to both married and unmarried people.

The institutions of marriage and the family, including the extended family, are the schools of intimacy—from kindergarten to graduate school.

Marriage and the family involve challenging relationships requiring strong identities, clear roles, and extensive relationship skills. These relationships cannot be discarded without serious consequences and carry major responsibilities, yet can be remarkably rewarding.

Among various illusions about marriage are: (1) marriage itself is to blame for relationship problems; (2) there is rarely a happy marriage; (3) fulfillment can be found primarily outside the family; and (4) only inadequate persons would devote their best efforts to home responsibilities.

The family is the only truly universal human institution. There are societies without religion, without formal education, without legal systems, even without formal economic systems. There is, however, no recorded instance of a society or culture without the family.[1] The family is the largest special interest group on the planet. If we take the world's population as four billion and arbitrarily divide by six (two parents and four children), there are nearly 700,000,000 families—more families than members of any religion or any nation except possibly China. There is simply nothing larger, more encompassing, or more powerful in human behavior than the family and its consequences, whether benevolent or detrimental.

Marriage and the family are not on trial, but how our society views and uses them is. Some professionals have seen so much pain and tragedy in certain families that they have erroneously diagnosed the problem to be the institutions of marriage and the family. They have also failed to understand the crucial distinction between intimate union and mere cohabitation. Much of their criticism of family per se should be aimed at distortions, abuses, and deviations in the "families" which merely cohabit.

A further error has been a preoccupation with the middle-class nuclear family and its weaknesses, seeing that isolated unit, rather than the extended family with its greater resources and flexibility, as *the* family model. Felix Uzoka, a Nigerian psychologist who has studied Western societies, in "The Myth of the Nuclear Family," is also concerned about the American assumption that "family" means two parents and children only. He reminds us that this middle-class view conflicts with world-wide reality where, in almost all cultures, the family is a large and extended network of interested and supportive aunts, uncles, grandparents, and other relatives. This limited idea, that the nuclear family is the model, has created a spiral of damage as professional and government therapeutic programs pour more effort into helping an isolated and fragile unit remain isolated. "Modern western parents who subscribe uncritically to the myth are overburdened and overwhelmed, and grandparents and relatives remain underemployed and are often lonely," Uzoka notes. "Surrogate social agencies (foster homes, etc.) have not been effective alternatives."[2] Further isolation has been promoted by an intrusive army of professionals, many of whom interfere with family relationships rather than strengthen them.

An example is the family therapist who weekly demonstrates in group therapy that he or she, not the parents, is in control.

Families have enormous power to help and even heal. I know one family of married children and parents who, in addition to their usual holiday contacts, have an annual business meeting and reunion. At one such meeting one of the married couples reported that they had had a difficult financial year and had been obliged to borrow money. Their report came from a general discussion of the economy and was not intended to solicit help. Nevertheless, afterward two different family members offered help.

While financial help is a common form of family support, there are others. Grandparents attend grandchildren's school plays, sisters-in-law listen sympathetically to each other's problems, and cousins become particular friends.

The special investment the family can make, even in distant relatives, is impressive. In one situation a harmless but mentally damaged older man was rescued from lonely flophouses and taken into his third cousin's family. In another situation, two children, eight and five, were taken from their parents' custody by court order. For some time they were shifted from foster home to foster home. Finally, after a thorough search for relatives, a married cousin was found some distance away. Neither the cousin nor his wife and children had ever met the two children. Through professional help designed to unite rather than replace families, the children were placed in their cousin's home where they stayed until they married, more secure and healthy than they could have been in a succession of well-meaning but non-relative foster homes.

It is within our families, growing up as children and observing our relatives, that we draw our first conclusions about marriage. Our reactions to the reality of our own marriage are largely influenced by the quality of our preparations for it. If we have experienced self-focused gratification and have exploited people to serve our appetites, marriage can be—and usually is

—a startling awakening as the illusion of self-gratification evaporates under the reality of our spouse's needs. If, on the other hand, our previous experiences have included respect for self and others, marriage can be the means through which unparalleled intimacy is achieved.

Marriage is the bonding of two clear and distinct entities. The wing of an airplane is *married* to the fuselage. The outer skin of a skyscraper is *married* to the inner framework. If either element were weakened, the result would be catastrophic. This is just as valid in the *marriage* of human beings. Benevolent marriage is both a bonding and an expansion of identity, the beginning of a human nuclear fusion which results in endless growth of identity. When identity is repressed, then intimacy has been violated. *Family*, like *marriage*, is just a word unless intimacy bonds the people involved. If this union does not occur between husband and wife, between parents and children, then they are experiencing cohabitation, not marriage or family life.

Realities of Marriage

Some consider even the mention of duties, responsibilities, and obligations tiresome. They want a relationship to be exuberant, bright, and nondemanding, an entertaining presentation of public selves. But an intimate relationship is immeasurably more substantial. It is earned after diligent effort. This seems drudgery to some—and it often is. It seems difficult—and it is. Those who never experience the complete process will never know the rewards of enduring long enough to build the foundation of lasting marriage. Many critics have not experienced, or even observed, the completion of marriage. They know only short-term relationships, painfully terminated marriages, or superficial cohabitations. Yet how reliable is the judgment of those who see only beginnings, never endings? Can they understand the benevolent consequences of relationships which have expanded and deepened over several decades when they have seen mainly those which have ended after a few months or years and often where mutual selfishness, not commitment, was the dominant tone?

In benevolent marriage, a complete, enduring relationship adds dimensions to life which are virtually indescribable—not because they are vague but because they are sacred. This type of marriage is not known to the merchandisers of appetite. Those who know the realities of benevolent married intimacy speak sparingly and discreetly because their experiences are too precious to chatter about carelessly or even share with serious researchers. For example, studies done by Kinsey, Masters and Johnson, and other well-known sexologists have been justly criticized because an important segment of the general population has consistently preferred not to discuss their private sexual behavior with researchers.[3] Thus, with a few exceptions, most sexual studies deal primarily with the attitudes and behaviors of people who *want* to reveal their private sexual behavior. The results, needless to say, have led to widespread biases. A complete reading of Kinsey or Masters and Johnson shows that their research subjects and methods focus on erotic activity, not on intimate relationships. Unfortunately, many professionals have drawn assumptions about intimate marital and family relationships from these narrow research efforts.

For example, one college text describes "most marriages which last more than five or ten years" as "unstable-satisfactory," because, "though the spouses believe they have a comfortable relationship, their disappointment with each other on occasion is obvious. In time of stress, hostility and buried resentment emerge. There are periodic outbursts of subtle or open aggression. The spouses attack each other emotionally and inflict fresh wounds. Some of the wounds heal; and even though scabbing and scarring occur the marriage remains basically sound."[4]

This definition might not seem unusual to any veteran of marriage; however, it must be compared to an "almost hypothetical" type of marriage these same authors call "stable-satisfactory." "Such a harmonious and collaborative union has seldom been directly observed by the authors, and then only between *elderly men and women* who have been married for thirty or more years. . . . We have never observed a generally constant collaborative union between spouses during the period when they are raising children." (Italics added.)[5]

These marriages, the authors of the college text declare, are so rare that the chances of younger couples attaining such qualities are "exceedingly slim." In their pessimism, however, these writers reveal both the narrowness of their experience and their research bias. If they had studied the beginnings of "stable-satisfactory" marriages, they would almost certainly have found them emerging from the stress, effort, and commitment of "unstable-satisfactory" marriages. It is precisely this reality which underscores the importance of the process of marriage—and not just our own marriages, but the cumulative effect over several generations of our parents' and grandparents' marriages. We are not good or evil in one generation. We learn, over time and over generations, the sum of the intimacies—the consequences of commitment—which lead to a full marriage. Thus it is alarming that the process of investing in marriage and family is being dismissed today by those who ignore available data about the consequences of discontinuity in the family.

The significance of understanding marriage *over time* was not apparent to me early in my career. But now that I have known several client couples for a decade or more, I realize that they have changed significantly since early marriage. One of the most important differences is that they have learned to handle conflict. Lewis Coser says that the closer or more intimate people are to each other the greater chance there is for conflict and, if it occurs, the greater the conflict will be. But he also asserts that some people who feel their relationship is strong will openly engage in occasional conflict rather than fearing it as they strive to clarify their relationship.[6]

Only recently a couple whom I have known for ten years "hit their stride" after a fairly turbulent beginning. Over time they have each learned to appreciate the other's personality;

they have learned which moods lead to strife and which call for empathy. Larry has become more appreciative of Elizabeth's intellect and she has learned to respect his emotions. It has taken them a long, long time to get to know and enjoy each other. Even so, they both report that it was well worth the struggle because of the depth and intensity of their intimacy and companionship. Today they are a very happy couple. Yet if their early marriage had been studied without reference to its direction it might have been accurately termed "unstable-unsatisfactory."

Because marriage is a vast subject, let us consider three aspects in assessing its realities: duration, the woman's dilemma, and the indentured employee-parent.

Duration

Throughout Judeo-Christian history, most people considered marriage permanent. Even troubled marriage was expected to endure. This does not excuse the low quality of many of these marriages. It is simply an observation of a cultural norm. Today, however, marriage is considered impermanent, its breakup an almost completely unilateral decision. This shift of opinion is important. If a society decided that honesty, protection of life, or the integrity of the financial system were temporary, to be preserved only until individuals became weary of their obligations, then almost any observer would predict a serious tearing of that society's fabric. Yet in our society, the most basic contract of all, marriage, is increasingly viewed as temporary, to be terminated for self-focused reasons like convenience, boredom, or personality difference. According to this doctrine, society has fewer and fewer rights and interests in the stability of marriages.

This attitude no doubt emerged out of the myth of the romantic marriage—a particularly cruel illusion—that is decidedly exploitive and determinedly self-focused. Romance as portrayed in contemporary media, particularly in "personality" magazines, is actually the process of picking someone who will gratify one's appetites. In the typical romantic approach, the male suitor (and lately some females) sorts through various potential mates for one whose appearance and role performance make *him* feel good, whose emotional repertoire gives *him* pleasure, and whose other traits promise *him* a reasonable fulfilling marital experience. It is little wonder that feminists challenge this approach; it is chauvinism personified. Yet the situation will hardly improve if women adopt the same ruthless approach. Obviously both men and women need to move beyond the illusions of romanticism. Another reason for abandoning the illusion of romance is its irresponsibility: it justifies dissolving the relationship once the "thrill" is gone. Some people eliminate the legal complications of abandonment by living together without marriage until the arrangement becomes inconvenient. My clinical experience suggests that the decision is seldom mutual. One partner leaves; the other suffers.

The net effect of this so-called romance has been to extinguish real love. Medical researcher James Lynch concludes in *The Broken Heart:* "There is a widespread belief in our modern culture that *love* is a word which has no meaning. A whole generation of detached, independent, self-sufficient, noncommitted individuals agree . . . that no one really needs to get hurt in modern human relationships. You can be intimate with someone and then leave, and nothing bad will happen."[7]

In our impatience to avoid the pain of unhealthy and unhappy marriages, we have attacked marriage itself, not the unhealthiness, and are only now beginning to realize that the side-effects of this kind of experimentation are as hazardous to human beings as the side-effects of thalidomide, the Pill, and pollution. Such impatience may be exhilarating, but it is also a dangerous way to tamper with humanity. Our "liberated" culture is less than a half-century old, a light weight indeed to set against millennia of institutionalized marriage. We have not yet felt the full consequence of anti-intimacy on the family. Arno Karlen compares ancient Rome and our day on the subjects of marriage, the family, and the roles of men and women:

> Like their modern American counterparts, Roman women suffered because they had cast off standards of femininity, but had nothing to take their place. . . . The idea of a satisfying life centered not on family and vocational involvement, but on pleasure and passion —whose satisfaction does not seem enough to anchor most people's sense of identity in the long run.
>
> Family and parental roles probably lost importance and clarity. . . . Judging by what psychiatrists [of today] see . . . one would expect certain characteristics to appear [in the Roman family and personality]. . . . The lack of dependable, warm, nurturing parents may produce children with frozen emotions . . . people who are cold and conscienceless. Parents whose sexual identity is shaky may produce children with poorly defined sexual identities. . . . Roman life was, in fact, marked by bisexuality, homosexuality, brutality and emotional caprice.[8]

It would defy reality to urge that every marriage absolutely must remain formally intact. There are marriages so sick and damaging that they would destroy everyone involved unless the spouses either changed dramatically or divorced. That is a sad but true fact of life. However, a point which bears repeating is the attitude with which people enter marriage. If two people marry tentatively then they are agreeing to withhold emotional and intellectual investment in their relationship. This emotional caution puts the partners on trial, exaggerates conflict, and undervalues harmony. Ill health in the spouse will become a burden, rather than an opportunity to nurture. Financial and emotional resources will be spent on immediate pleasures, not investments in future enjoyments or security.

When two people enter marriage with a profound and serious commitment, then when they cope with conflict, health, finances, and the myriad other facets of intimate life, these become milestones of progress rather than barriers to personal gratification. They renew their commitments again and again as their marriage encounters inevitable challenges.

My alarm is not that some marriages fail. That will be a fact of life until we are all perfect. My alarm arises from beliefs, entertainments, research conclusions, even laws which prevent good marriages from being achieved. For example, in Denver and Seattle, public monies have provided counseling and financial support for divorced people. An editorial in *Social Work* finds apparent correlation between tax-based financial assistance and increased divorce and family weakness. It queries: "There is a potentially insidious quality to these services. By assuming the responsibilities for emotional adjustments and even economic support, thereby making the consequences of a divorce a little less painful, are these services also making its occurrence a little more likely? . . . By reducing the level of anguish among the divorced population, the number of future divorces might increase, subsequently increasing the sum of suffering in society."[9]

This does not mean that a family forced to stay intact by economic pressure is necessarily a happy one. However, I claim that institutionalized human social bonds, especially families, are the workground from which intimate relationships develop. The weight and stability of traditional social covenants encourage us to remain enduringly committed to each other despite the distractions of triumph and trial. And it is in society's interest to reinforce these covenants.

Consider some data collected by Lynch about the effect of enduring marriage on health and longevity. He concludes that "a person's life may be shortened by the lack of human companionship," after considering an impressive quantity of data, among them:

—The low Japanese heart disease rate is usually attributed to low cholesterol in the diet; Lynch points out that it relates even more closely to the virtually nonexistent divorce rate and the social stability in Japan.

—Irish men who migrated to the United States had two to six times more heart disease than their brothers who stayed in Ireland, even though the Irish consumed five hundred or more calories per day of rich food with saturated fats. A primary social difference was a very low divorce rate and strong ties within the families in Ireland.

—In general, unmarried people in the United States die twenty-five times more frequently from causes other than old age than married people.

—Every listed cause of death in the period 1959-1961 for the United States was lower for married than for single, divorced, or widowed men; this included heart disease, cancer, suicide, and homicide. The same pattern also generally held for women.

—Every industrialized nation has similar mortality patterns for unmarried people, despite cultural differences.

—In residential institutions such as mental hospitals and prisons, bachelors comprise twenty-one times more of the population than married men do.

—Married men have fifty percent fewer chronic diseases which limit their activities.

—Divorce for white males in the period 1940-1960 "precisely mirrored the coronary death pattern" for the twenty-five- to forty-four-year-old age group, wherein marriages began in 1940.

—Suicide is higher for single people: three times higher than for married women, four times higher than for married men.[10]

Another analysis of the benefits of an enduring family lifestyle is provided by Victor Fuchs, who compared rates of death, crime, divorce, mobility, and so forth, in two neighboring states, Utah and Nevada. Nevada had the highest negative rates (death, divorce) in the Intermountain West, and Utah had the lowest. He hypothesized that Utah, due to its family/marriage values and practices, provided a milieu in which people were healthier and lived with fewer symptoms of despair. Nevada, with much higher degrees of mobility, family breakdown, and social alienation, was a decidedly unhealthy and despairing place to live, despite the high income and educational levels of its population.[11]

Despite the obvious benefits to a social structure from encouraging healthy, stable family relationships, American culture seems to be pursuing almost suicidal policies. Men's needs for intimacy have been under attack ever since the image of the virile male, always competent and emotionally reserved, first gained credence. Now, women's intimate needs are being assaulted by a tidal wave of social change, some of it beneficial but much of it deadly.

The Woman's Dilemma

American women face a dilemma created today by two extreme viewpoints. One extreme demands that women find identity outside the home—at work, in civic activities, or through a college degree; those who "stay at home" fail to "realize their potential." The other extreme requires that a woman subordinate herself to husband, children, and housekeeping, or if unmarried, remain wistfully "unfulfilled" while working at a job that will keep her minimally self-sufficient while she pursues her real career of "waiting."

These two positions present women with two wrong answers to the questions of establishing healthy relationships, and eventually intimacy. Ironically, American men have faced the same dilemma for years, attacked as not being "serious" about their careers if they put family needs first, accused, especially recently, of being negligent fathers if they put careers first. Traditionally, it must be admitted, many men have felt freer to emphasize careers because they have been financially supporting full-time adults—their wives—to take care of their children, but such an approach has never answered the question of whether it is the best decision for the children.

Today at least, both men and women share a dubious equality of frustration; to be a mature, fulfilled adult with a sense of identity, developing competence in relationship skills, rewarding intimate relationships, and a satisfying sense of using talents in the service of others, must a person choose between marriage-children and community-career? The very phrasing of the choice as an either-or ultimatum betrays its weakness, especially since adherents to one extreme are likely to deny any fulfillment at all in the other position. Such stridency only confuses the issue.

By discussing the woman's challenge perhaps the man's can also be better understood.

One of the most frequent indictments that many concerned people share is the view that women are generally victimized by marriage:

> Mothers of young children, in particular, lead a sharply restricted life. . . . When the children grow older her world broadens more, perhaps through returning to work or participating in community activities. Nevertheless, since childbearing is still considered to be more the mother's obligation than the father's [the author does not explain how childbearing can ever become a male function] her own development as a distinctive personality slows down. Instead her satisfactions come from her contributions to the happiness and success of her husband and children. . . .
>
> While some young women use the designation Ms., they ordinarily assume the husband's name, in effect becoming a less distinctive individual.[12]

There is evidence that certain types of marriage do stultify women—and men, too. However, in the enduring, benevolent marriage we are discussing, the two companions learn very early that the terms *breadwinner* and *housewife* are illusory, that new terms are needed. The very term *housewife* implies that a woman's primary relation is with a house, not with a home. The man who massages his ego through his employment, who leaves his mind at the office, who lavishes material things on his wife in place of his time and attention, may be a breadwinner, but he also exploits the human being to whom he is married. If his wife accepts this state of affairs, she either learns to find affection from children, friends, or other family members while stifling her resentment and sadness, or she learns to exploit him.

Somewhere along the way they strike a "yours-mine" bargain. They both fulfill culturally acceptable roles, but neither is committed to building a life together; they cohabit, but neither is a homebuilder.

With homebuilding marriages, the identities, roles, and relationships move the two companions toward each other. Mutual respect for uniqueness strengthens identities. The weaknesses of two, modified by the strengths of two, expand roles. Relationship skills grow as life's challenges are dealt with together. Two people engage in different activities, orbiting around the common nucleus of creating a home. When these experiences are allowed to deteriorate to roles labeled *housewife* or *breadwinner*, then they have sunk to the lowest common denominator of exchanging cleaning services for paying the bills. This sterility has nothing to do with the rich, deep passions of real marriage.

More than once I have counseled women who gave up their own interests so completely to their husband and children that they eventually became pale images of their former selves. One especially sad situation occurred when a woman, Elsie, had helped her husband obtain a Ph.D. in chemistry by running a family business for many years. By the time he finished school, she was exhausted, virtually all of her own emotional reserves gone. By then, he found her boring and rather difficult. When he left, Elsie reacted not with anger but with devastating self-doubt. She tried to explain this tragedy as her own personal failure to please her husband. My assessment was that she had protected her husband so successfully from the realities of marriage and family life during the stress of graduate school that he had no investment in the relationship and no understanding of her heroic efforts. When she began to appreciate and value herself —and allow herself to feel accurate anger at her husband's betrayal—she was on the road toward a healthier self-image and the ability to understand both their failures.

In reassuring contrast was another couple. The husband also went through a long and demanding graduate program while the wife worked and managed the family. She also was exhausted but when she challenged the injustice of her husband's taking her sacrifices for granted, they stopped to evaluate their troubled marriage. In this case, they agreed that it was time for the wife to renew herself through enriching activity. The husband took care of the home and children weekly while his wife took an evening art class at the community college, and he arranged his weekend schedule so she could also spend several peaceful hours painting. She expanded herself mentally and increased her self-esteem. This was not "yours-mine": "he is a Ph.D. so I must become an artist." Rather it simply acknowledged that the get-an-education crisis was over and that burdens could now be redistributed.

I am encouraged by the loving realism of several married couples I have met recently—a new trend, I hope—who have thoughtfully assessed their goals for education and career in light of their abilities, limitations, desires, and resources and have made plans to meet these goals equitably, but always with the intimate needs of their own relationship and their children—present or future—foremost.

Husbands have traditionally been applauded for being breadwinners and little more. To be sure, going to work every day and coming home every day is one measure of commitment. Dependable breadwinners add immeasurably to the material security of marriage, family, and society. But steadily employed breadwinners are also rewarded in their egos and pocketbooks. When this commitment in one area is used to thrust all other marital and family demands onto the wife, she becomes an exploited victim deprived of social and emotional rewards. Some have argued that wives should have the psychological and financial rewards of paid employment, pointing to studies which conclude that employed mothers are happier than the stay-at-home variety. These conclusions deserve a closer look, even though the real issue is how society rewards—or, rather, fails to reward—good parenting by both fathers and mothers.

Unfortunately, that closer look often finds more heat than light. As Urie Bronfenbrenner has warned, the current state of research about the effects of "maternal employment or day care . . . as presently measured show trends that are inconsistent, ephemeral, and small in magnitude."[13] Gold and Andres conclude even more tellingly, "The relationship between maternal employment and children's development varies depending upon what aspects of development are studied."[14] This simply means that every marriage, family, and child is unique—hardly a Nobel-Prize discovery.

Let us look at our society's disparagement of nurturant roles more closely in light of the deep human need for intimacy. If one were simply dealing with societal evolution, then employing both parents outside the home is merely a trend with mainly economic and political meaning. But in reality it begs a larger question: "What contributes to healthy, happy individuals and families? And what fosters the development of human intimacy? In this light, the issue ceases to be women's "liberation" (giving them the privileges traditionally granted men). Instead the issue becomes the health of the whole family, recalling both mothers *and* fathers to those responsibilities and duties which create a climate for intimacy. It would be black humor, if it were not painful, that our day may see men, weary of the lonely workplace, groping toward the intimacy of family, while women, harrassed by economic or emotional disparagement of their nurturant role, grope toward the very illusions which men are abandoning. If this is so, where will the rising generation experience intimacy? Educators already report the struggles they have with alienated, rootless "latchkey children" who go home each day to an empty house. What price is being paid?

One family headed off a potential conflict by a joint recommitment of both husband and wife to homebuilding roles. They resolved the financial pressures by buying a smaller house and getting rid of the second car. Even though this family bulges the seams of the smaller house, they also have more family time because one parent, in this case the mother, was able to quit work. Bruised egos, talks after school, family meals, all have responded to a climate created by a mother with physical and emotional reserves to create stability rather than harried and tense "coping." The father works diligently for his employer but has time and energy to listen to, work with, and play with his family. They struggle with inflation and medical bills, but they do not struggle with the overwhelming weight of alienation through distraction.

Another father perceived some growing needs on the part of his twelve-year-old son. He requested release from a prestigious but time-consuming commitment as a lay officer in his local church congregation and accepted the much less prestigious position of Sunday School teacher. He feels that being able to spend time with his son and his son's friends was the key to preventing some problems of rebellion and experimentation before they developed too far.

I have sadly watched the opposite process also, the erosion of a marriage and family because of the parents' involvement outside the home. First, Bob began spending most evenings and weekends at work, "building a nest egg," he rather fiercely declared. Then Helen went into business with another woman. Soon the children were among the best dressed and most troubled in their neighborhood. It is too easy to blame materialism. The real culprit was that both parents avoided the responsibilities of intimacy with each other and with their children. Helen's and Bob's backgrounds had not prepared them to invest in and nurture each other, let alone their three vigorous children. Intelligent and hard-working people, they threw themselves into activities they could handle, especially employment outside the home. They could have lived on one salary, but they were afraid of the demands of each other and the children. My professional involvement was with two of their daughters whose needs for intimacy became so great that they broke moral and legal laws.

Perhaps our wisest course is to develop a healthy skepticism about experts and simply trust our observations of families in our own neighborhoods: children suffer when fathers neglect them and when mothers neglect them. Sometimes fathers and mothers, uncomfortable and unhappy in their parenting roles, use employment as an excuse for neglecting their children. Sometimes that excuse may instead be a hobby, a community cause, church service, or housecleaning—any excuse will do. Sometimes, circumstances require both parents to balance parenting and employment. Some do so, struggling to maintain a close marriage and a loving, effective style of parenting. No one solution will work for all families, but every successful family must find a way to create a climate in which intimacy—that most unrelenting of emotional needs—can flourish.

Certainly the burden of single parenthood imposes great strains on a mother or father who must meet both economic and nurturant needs for his or her children, and certainly no one would assume that burden lightly, for we have all seen men and women unable to bear it successfully and children who have suffered as a result. But certainly no one would assert that it is impossible to succeed as a single parent either.

All of these circumstances are complex and emotional. Many men, women, and children have been victimized by a system that worked to benefit someone else at their expense. I acknowledge and regret that pain. But here we must resolutely remember that we are talking about what enhances the development of intimacy and refuse to be diverted by the red herrings of power politics, dramatic social issues, economic influence, and sociological studies of varying value, no matter how tempting. The fact is that our culture, suicidally, seldom values or rewards good parenting. Women who want to be good mothers and men who want to be good fathers must develop the strength and inner resources to be upstream swimmers, accepting the fact that they will be sometimes misunderstood, pitied, or even mocked.

Both pro and con camps have debated the wrong question: material and intellectual satisfaction, rather than the higher common denominator of intimacy. The pro-employment camp demands that a woman place herself outside the home and there be guaranteed satisfaction. The anti-employment faction demands that a woman chain herself to home and there be guaranteed satisfaction. The debate is over an illusion, not a reality. If we need a precedent, look at the men who drive themselves for vocational prestige yet by their single-mindedness lose the affection of the only people who might be interested in them for nonmaterialistic reasons. It is highly unlikely that a mother devoting all her time and energy to her husband and children has ever existed. Indeed, the historical period is very brief and very recent during which mothers have not been involved in many tasks besides giving direct attention to spouse and children.

The experts have certainly been wrong before. The past generation's human behavior experts who prescribed the nuclear family as the norm created an anxious generation of parents who saw their children as their complete universe. Now another generation's experts are saying that, contrary to "tradition" (whose?), wives and mothers have many interests and Johnny and Susie need sufficient room to grow.

One wonders if a pre-twentieth-century wife and mother would not wonder what the fuss is all about. Of course a woman who waits on her child hand and foot is dissatisfied, and of course her child will most likely become an unpleasant monster. Of course it is ridiculous for a woman to send her children off to school and then anesthetize her mind with soap operas because "good mothers stay home." A similar illusion confuses husband-wife relationships. Men do enjoy various activities outside the home, and their daily life is enhanced by them. But many men also strongly desire to have all these activities revolve around a secure and predictable home and family.

Real life does not permit a marital relationship of undistracted attention to each other's needs. To exclude all other experiences has never been possible, or for that matter desirable. Sheldon Vanauken, in his autobiography, *A Severe Mercy,* told how he and his wife, Jean, decided early to exclude any competitors for each other's attention. With youthful certitude, they decided that religion and children must not threaten their relationship. But as they matured, they discovered unexpected hungers. Both accepted religion, but Vanauken's vasectomy precluded children, a deprivation which they mourned too late. Then, still young, Jean died. A grief-stricken Vanauken wrote to their friend C. S. Lewis, a Christian philosopher, in search of consolation. With an eye on the consequences, Lewis rebuked the folly of Vanauken's tampering with reality. He took a philosopher's approach to voluntary sterility, asking how the pagans, then the Stoics, would see it:

> Then come to Christians. They wd.* of course agree that man & wife are "one flesh"; they wd. perhaps admit that this was most admirably realised by Jean and you. But surely they wd. add that this One Flesh must not (and in the long run cannot) "live to itself" any more than the single individual. . . . (The idea behind your voluntary sterility, that an experience, e.g. maternity, wh. cannot be shared shd. on that account be avoided, is surely v[ery] unsound. For *a.* (forgive me) the conjugal act itself depends on opposite, reciprocal and therefore unshare-able experiences. Did you want her to feel she had a *woman* in bed with her? *b.* The experience of a woman denied maternity is one you *did not & could not* share with her. To be denied paternity is different, trivial in comparison. [Most fathers would challenge this assertion.]
>
> One way or another the thing had to die. Perpetual springtime is not allowed. You were not cutting the wood of life according to the grain. There are various possible ways in wh. it cd. have died tho' both the parties went on living. You have been treated with a severe mercy.[15]

As Lewis carefully points out, when people make decisions about marriage and family issues, the consequences are human realities, not just abstract preferences. He saw the contradiction of trying to preserve intimacy by limiting those who might lay primary claim to it. In contrast, I remember a young couple who

---

* Lewis abbreviated considerably in his personal correspondence.

sacrificed a great deal—the wife's education, movies, a car, a comfortable home, new clothes, even an occasional dinner out—and lived on the husband's scholarship while having four babies in five years because *both* agreed profoundly that they wanted children as well as a trade school diploma for the husband. Even though their assignments were very different during those five years, they both felt that they were performing equally important functions, functions that the other understood, respected, and needed as much as the one accomplishing the task. The fact that such maturity of goals and skill in communication is rare does not make their achievement any less attainable for others. By putting their home and children first, they were signalling that whatever piano lessons, church activities, night classes, and social life came later would be truly enriching, not an emotional and social flight from intimacy. And they were telling their children that they were more valuable than the people and commitments outside the family. In a happy home where children are future parents, how better can they learn than by seeing their own parents make the choice that loved ones come first, though not necessarily exclusively?

Many children of this generation are learning from their parents that their highest priority should be intellectual and financial achievement through activities outside the home. One study of maternal employment concluded with chilling logic that since home is not as important as it used to be, we ought to raise children who will be prepared to concentrate even more on work.[16] If this decision were implemented, it would have the effect of lessening the importance of homebuilding with each succeeding generation until marriage and family would become a matter of public policy, shaped by professionals and legislated by government for the cold technicalities of social order.

What then is the solution? The either-or debate between home and work has obscured the fact that there are other options. We need not claim—for it certainly could not be proved—that all satisfaction lies in either place. If the home is the emotional base of operations and the center of interest and attention, then both men and women will voluntarily give it their best efforts. Thus employment, civic responsibilities, religious duties, recreation, and many other homebuilding activities will grow spontaneously out of that values system, supporting and enhancing the home.

Each couple must look realistically at the consequences of the choices they have made and are making. I think again of Bob and Helen. They decided to concentrate on employment, an area where they both already knew they were competent, rather than on building intimacy with each other and their children, an area where they felt less skilled and where the outcome was less predictable. That decision, though, resulted in very predictable problems.

But recognizing these consequences does not solve the problem. It is not likely that Bob and Helen can immediately become warm, nurturing people by wishing it or that their teenage children will promptly respond. In some ways, Bob and Helen need to be taught all over again about loving—and that will come best from their own parents and extended family. The healing process is long, though a change in direction can come dramatically while they relearn—or learn for the first time—the skills of intimacy rather than the skills of the marketplace.

The Indentured Employee-Parent

During the seventeenth and eighteenth centuries, impoverished British subjects could purchase passage to the American and Australian colonies by agreeing to indenture themselves as servants for a specified number of years. They temporarily traded freedom for the chance of later freedom. Psychologically, our economic system operates in much the same way, contracting with an employee to buy his time for the money that will give him later freedom—not only from want but also for leisure.

In many ways, our economic system is inherently abusive, a reality we must acknowledge even while we appreciate its openness and opportunities. Many jobs are boring and spiritually stultifying. Some professions ruthlessly demand that personal and family interests come second. Some employment, while honorable and essential, offers meagre rewards (school teachers) while others are comparatively nonessential yet offer extravagant rewards (professional athletes). Our system makes it difficult for the young and the old to find honorable, rewarding work that is suited to their limited capacities. By separating the workplace from the home, children cannot learn employment skills from their parents. By emphasizing financial rather than human contracts, it deemphasizes human values and human relationships. The deep joy that comes from working at challenging tasks which stretch one's capacities, enlarge and stimulate one's mind, and reward one's attempts are limited to comparatively few.

However, the justice or injustice of our economic system is a subject for other books. We cannot deal here with the many workers—perhaps the majority—who diligently and faithfully work at less than fulfilling jobs to support those they love, making a daily sacrifice because of that love. Instead, we will here discuss those who voluntarily indenture themselves: the woman whose husband earns an adequate, though perhaps not lavish, income; the husband or single person who defines success and personal worth in terms of income, prestige, and recognition rather than by the quality of his or her human relationships.

If we keep that context—human intimacy—in mind, however, it almost immediately shows us one flaw in the satisfaction studies currently popular about employed mothers these days. These studies generally assume and find that certain satisfactions are more quickly and easily obtained through employment than through family. Without question, husband and children make heavy emotional and energy demands on the woman—as wife and children do on a man. Marriage and family are life-long processes, never finished, always changing with moods, health, age, and myriad other circumstances. At the office, job descriptions are specific, usually written; union or government rules decree coffee breaks, starting and quitting times, and lunch breaks; social and emotional interchanges are clearly defined and seldom demanding; people dress nicely and usually make an effort to be courteous and pleasant. For this the woman is paid money and can buy things. And except for the very nurturant care and teaching of youngsters in school, there are no recorded instances of management requiring an employee to wipe co-workers' runny noses, feed them, wash their clothes, or explain their bad performance to the stockholders. While a mother's unpaid work really is never done, an employee's is. This short-term reward is very real.

A recent magazine article was illustrated by a photograph of a woman at a business desk with a baby in a highchair near her. With phone in one hand and baby bottle in the other, the woman portrayed a dilemma. Her eyes, body, and attention were focused on the inanimate—hence, controllable—objects on her desk and away from the baby, who could not quite reach the bottle.[17] Within the same article, the director of a research institute devoted to women's issues commented worriedly on the trend at its sponsoring university, where women were earning degrees in "female" professions such as "education, home economics, and health but [were] behind in business and management, mathematics and physical science."[18]

We will not discuss here the solution many women seek—that of combining a career with motherhood. Some of them, particularly those with supportive husbands, may find apparent success. Nor will we deal with the fact that increasing numbers of single mothers—regardless of preference—find themselves obliged to combine the two. The consequences of these two cases must be studied over the next two generations. Instead we will discuss the political rhetoric and apparently scientific studies that combine to show full-time mothering, when that choice is possible, as less honored and less inviting than employment.

Sadly, many women find escape to the office an illusion within an illusion. Most working women, like most working men, will likely have marginal jobs with marginal pay and marginal satisfactions. Very few working people of either sex sit at large desks and enjoy high status, flexible hours, and lavish salaries; .002 percent of the general population are attorneys, .04 percent are business managers and .0011 percent are life and physical scientists.[19] Women's percentage of prestigious jobs is even less. Even if women could be granted 50 percent representation in high prestige professions, the majority of working women (and men) would still have grinding, boring, and marginal employment.

When we ask, then, what women seek from outside employment, we must also ask what the enduring hopes and satisfactions of working *men* are and what people need to make life full and benevolent.

Immediately before and after World War II, researchers uncovered a factor about employee motivation which was startling then but has become common knowledge today. It is that money and job titles are less motivating than self-esteem and informal structure. Current Japanese management methods, which have helped capture the electronics and automotive markets, only formalized such effective and informal American systems as small work groups, supervisor-employee interchanges, and benevolent company interest in the employee's total life.[20]

Refined research since the 1940s has gone further and found that job satisfaction is correlated to general life satisfaction instead of the other way around. People who enjoy self-esteem and secure marital and family relationships are more likely to be secure and effective employees.[21]

If this is so—and it does appear to be true—our society faces a most appalling possibility. As intimacy within family dwindles and as emotional reliance upon one's job and coworkers increases, then the time may well come when intimate human needs could exceed the capacity of society to provide for them. Such a possibility would make the dark ages seem brilliant by comparison.

As I have talked with women friends and clients who voluntarily seek employment away from their young children, I have observed that many seem motivated by a fear of intimacy. They substitute the emotionally less demanding experiences of employment for the much more challenging experiences of intimacy within the family as did Bob and Helen.[22] By leaving the house—and therefore husband and children—a woman is able to control her daily schedule, get material reinforcement for self-focused identity and role (clothes, cars, vacations, her "own" spending money), and use relationship skills which are far less demanding than those required at home. True, she achieves equality with many men, but these men, emotionally undernourished and miserly nurturers, are not desirable models for anyone, including their own children.

I encountered the depressing consequences of this life-style in Otto, who had tried to commit suicide by an overdose of medication. Other occupants of his boarding house missed him at the morning meal and called the ambulance. Otto's stomach was successfully pumped and his physical life saved. Emotionally, however, he had died several months earlier.

Otto's story was all too familiar. From the beginning of his marriage, he had given almost all his energy and time to his work, as was expected of a "responsible" husband and father. After the children were all in school, his wife went back to college, obtained a degree, and entered her own profession.

About the time his wife was achieving success in her profession Otto sustained an injury that forced an early but well-paid retirement. Within months his presence, as a virtual stranger, so irritated his wife and children that they moved to another state. Otto's pleas were in vain. Eventually, deeply depressed without family or work, he tried to kill himself.

Because I do not want to repeat Otto's mistake, I do not want to forget the pathetic scene I saw the day I helped Otto home from the hospital. He directed me to a very old rooming house in a decaying part of town. We trudged up rickety stairs and opened a stale room, furnished with one chair, an ancient bed, and a table lamp. I did not want to stay because it hurt and I did not want to leave for the same reason. To this day I see Otto seated on his bed as I closed the thin door.

Studies on the consequences of putting employment ahead of family life are still too sparse for us to comfortably conclude that this social trend is merely mildly interesting. I believe it will prove to be devastating.

When choices are made in early marriage which destroy intimacy, when fathers and mothers refuse to invest their hearts in the lives of their children, the consequences are extensive and ominous. Cornell psychologist and researcher Urie Bronfenbrenner exhaustively analyzed the 1970 census data. He found that over the past twenty-five years mothers have left home so often that neither parent is available much anymore. In 1975, 54 percent of American mothers with children ages six to seventeen worked, as did nearly 33 percent with children under three. In 1974, about one million children lived with only one parent. Bronfenbrenner further observes that "there has also been a sharp decline in the amount of attention that one or both parents give to affectionate child raising," even when parents and children are with each other, and cites death and violence as part of the price of this alienation. Seventeen nations have better infant mortality prevention than does the United States. One out of nine American teenagers appears in juvenile courts for crimes, including dramatically increasing personal violence and property vandalism. In twenty years, the suicide rate has tripled for youths fifteen to nineteen years of age. Scholastic aptitude tests have steadily declined. Bronfenbrenner's concern is explicit: "The healthy growth of each child requires a commitment of love, care, and attention from someone . . . but most of the enduring, irrational involvement and intimate activities must come from parents. . . . *A second cause is our socio-technical structure* . . . that conduce[s] us to separate and fragment rather than come together."[23] The 1980 data had not been analyzed at this writing but no one expects reverses of these statistics of isolation and loneliness.

We have not yet learned that intimacy and all its rewards cannot coexist with self-focused behavior. As women and men redefine their roles—a right they certainly have—they must do so with a knowledge of reality—of real causes and real effects, of real consequences for real decisions. Some things are possible and some are not. One of our grave challenges is to help a generation of human beings acquire a sense of self-esteem, security, and trust without two parents committed to homebuilding and at least one parent available most of the time. It begs the question to point to the divorce rate and say that the single-parent family is the trend of the future. So was polio until the virus which caused it was conquered.

Signs of a quiet revolution among men are refusals to relocate, avoidance of evening and weekend work, and so forth. Such new priorities are encouraging. Those who scorn the homebuilders—both men and women—reveal their own lack of wisdom, their ignorance of their own debt to the past, and their own lack of faith in the future. Loving, homebuilding mothers and fathers practice psychology, sociology, political science, economics, medicine, and business management. They heal, defend, tutor, and anchor the minds and hearts of their spouses and children. The fact that some marriages and families have failed does not repeal the benevolence of intact, healthy marriages and families.

It is tempting to express anger at critics of homebuilders, especially critics of women who choose that role. Surely fairness would demand that they grant their sisters the same rights of choice they so zealously claim for themselves. It is also tempting to compare the respective duties of the two types of role preferences and risk comparing their respective relationship skills. One might also raise the question of the real, enduring intimacies which are possible in the two life-styles.

At least part of my anger at critics of the homebuilder-wife or homebuilder-husband is based upon the example of one whose efforts I have now observed for nearly a quarter of a century within my own home. Compassionate and wise, she touches many lives and her advice is sought by teenagers and adults. She has granted me the reality of fatherhood by six difficult pregnancies, each child mutually desired and welcomed. She was actively involved in every one of the ten different schools the children have thus far attended and has negotiated innumerable parent-teacher conferences. She reads challenging books continually, holds two assignments in her church, and coordinates six-day-a-week training for a profoundly retarded child. She overcame the city council's objections to a school crossing guard, served on a citizen's zoning committee, and sat as a juror during the same period. She feeds the pets, plants the tulip bulbs, and each day nurtures friends who telephone or visit her. She shops sales, sews, bakes bread from flour she grinds, and bottles fruit for storage and economy. Within this schedule she votes at every election, sharing her insightful study of community issues. Most recently, she again put the family's needs ahead of her own by relocating, separating herself with real pain from deep-rooted friends and leaving behind her first grandchild.

It is arrogant nonsense to imply that this woman who has voluntarily chosen her home and family as her highest priorities is inadequate or narrow or lacks the courage to engage life. It is offensive when writers, whose worlds are voluntarily circumscribed by the workplace, challenge the meaning of a homebuilder's soul-stretching, spirit-deepening life. The intelligently committed wife and mother—homebuilder—knows a world unknown to those who would call her a less distinctive individual.

Conclusion

There is little doubt that women and men are trying desperately to redefine their roles. How tragic if illusions are used as guidelines for such efforts! How encouraging if basic realities form the foundation for harmonious union! Marriages and families are successful to the degree that they enhance the identities of the members. Commitment to one another within marriage and family, in preference to outside distractions, is actually a covenant of mutual enhancement. Thus, identities, roles, and relationship skills become complementary and reinforcing, not because it is easy but because it is the family's commitment to do so. In this type of marriage or family there can be no second-class citizens. All have full citizenship. All are concerned about each other's well-being. The highest common denominator is benevolent intimacy.

There is no doubt that many marriages have been horribly destructive, that many families have bred disturbed, tragic children, and that women have been victims more frequently than men. However, these sad cases are evidences that there are sick elements in many marriages, not that marriage itself is sick. Beginning marriages which seek to enhance identity, refine crucial roles, and teach relationship skills for husband, wife, and children must, by their very nature, lead to benevolent consequences. Women who voluntarily abandon their marriages and families will only add to the chaos which so many men have created over the years by their unwillingness to be home-builders first. Nurturance and compassion are the highest common denominators of intimacy for both men and women. As the voices of women are heard with the respect they deserve in the larger community, the voices of men must also be heard with the frequency their wives and children need within the home. If this pattern—possible but threatened in our culture—does not become a wider reality, we will not be able to reverse the forces undermining families, and fewer unions will mature from their beginning state into the solidly committed security of an enduring marriage.

CHAPTER SIX

Enduring Marriage: The Illusion of Eroticism The Reality of Complete Intimacy

Newly married couples know little about deep and full emotional and physical intimacy, but ultimate intimacy will grow from self-discipline and knowledge. That is why marriage is essential, for gratification without commitment diminishes our capacity to experience and enjoy complete intimacy.

Emotional integrity over time leads to sexual fulfillment in marriage. It does not lead to excitement but rather to a security which may even appear dull to critics. Enduring marital intimacy is benevolent, providing the emotional, physical, and social stability which the institution of marriage was designed to bring about.

With a foundation of secure identities and clear but flexible roles, a couple can build upon their commitments to marriage and family to achieve sexual intimacy. Attempts to build unity from the foundation of sexual compatibility simply have it backwards. I am embarrassed to think that as a young counselor I agreed with one troubled couple who expressed optimism about their future because "our sex life is so exciting!" The rest of their marriage was filled with hatred, anger, emotional assaults, even physical attacks on each other. I now wish I had known enough to help them measure the price they paid in personal integrity each time they used their bodies for physical gratification and pseudo-reconciliation after vicious emotional experiences. They and I were sadly ignorant of the consequences of their behavior.

Sexual Ignorance

Ignorance about our bodies, our minds, and the consequences of sexual expression may be the greatest enemy of sexual intimacy. Yet in this open era of ours, outspokenness, even vulgarity, masquerade as knowledge and candor. It has been my observation that as two mature people expand their identities, their roles, and their relationship in marriage, they cherish more fervently and with increasing reverence the growing power of their passion. As their knowledge of each other and self increases, so does their respect for the value and privacy of human intimacy. Full sexuality, I contend, comes not in beginning marriage but when the relationship is firmly based on a foundation of identity, role, and relationship skills. In short, as the emotional marriage deepens so does physical intimacy.

Serious personal and marital damage has been caused over the centuries by ignorance about human sexuality. While behavioral scientists, schools, and even churches have urged parents to educate their children about sex, many parents feel deep reluctance to give graphic descriptions of sexual behavior, and that reticence is often mistaken for embarrassment. Without question some parents are rigidly uncomfortable with this subject, but many others are simply modest. After informed, careful thought, they decide that explicit discussions of sexual activity are not appropriate between anyone except married companions. For this modesty, they are criticized as too inhibited by people who often speak more crudely than sensitively about such an important subject.

Most people would grant that biological facts about physiology and body processes need to be made available to everyone. Accurate biological information, including charts and illustrations, is crucial and can be found in many good medical reference works or encyclopedias. Ideally, a well-informed parent could and should provide this information. But the frame of reference for this knowledge should be values like integrity, kindness, and reverence for the human body rather than a course in how to perform erotic acts. These values have everything to do with our sense of identity, or roles, and the skills we use in living with each other. Parents can and should teach these values, as concepts and by the example of their own relationship.

There is little evidence that a virginal couple need go to their honeymoon with anything more than correct biological information and such values as tenderness, consideration, and sensitivity to each other's needs. The remaining knowledge comes best from each other, no one else. Outsiders do not know what the two lovers know—and never can—for they, in the marvelously accurate biblical term, are to *know* each other.

Each newly married couple's first complete physical intimacy is unique. The combination of their bodies and their personalities are unlike anyone else's. If intimacy, not mere gratification, is sought, no other personal event should be so private and special as these first sharings, the disclosure of one's body to another, and the first complete physical giving and receiving in a unique and exclusive relationship. Their discovery of each other can be hampered by vain attempts to perform elaborate exercises in technical competence. For them, sexuality is not something you *do* but it is an important element of what they *are*: two committed, respecting, and loving companions.

Despite the outpourings of sexual information from the press, there is still some evidence that many married Americans feel that their sex lives together should begin as a sacredly private event and stay that way. The fact that most of our sexual data comes from people rather eager to talk about it means that the majority of the best-known reports contain major error and bias. The Kinsey Report was essentially drawn from people who preferred unusual and unconventional (though not necessarily deviant) behavior; the well-advertised Hite Report on female behavior (and now on male behavior) is extremely subjective and had only three thousand surveys returned of a hundred thousand sent out; the Hunt-*Playboy* report had a one-in-five return rate; and the Masters and Johnson data came from people who volunteered to perform sexually before observers in a laboratory with instruments attached to their bodies.[1] The values and character disparity between people who want to show or tell their sexual lives and those who will not is enormous. And claims that those who insist on privacy are really only repressed, yearning for uninhibited sex, remain opinion, not objectively measured fact.

Some clinical experiences have reinforced the values of privacy in sexual matters. The first involved a family devastated by an irresponsible therapist who had persuaded the parents to share the details of their sexual life with their teenage son. Even though the son was sexually experienced himself and rather outspoken, he reacted very negatively to the over-intense experience of dealing with his parents' sexuality and developed sexually oriented disturbances and fantasies. The parents divorced. The son's disturbance continued. Such exposure, clinically speaking, appeared to be an assault on the minds and personalities of all concerned.

The second situation involved a well-educated, strong-willed, and multi-talented woman, who sought counseling with her husband in an attempt to effect a reconciliation. Their disagreements centered on extensive sexual dysfunction, though neither was notably inhibited. Later, after reconciliation, this woman wrote to me: "I believe my friends and I contributed to my problems by open discussions of sex. It became so casual and commonplace that we all lost sight of its special qualities." Restoring sex to its "special" role for this woman and her husband accompanied the healing of their wounds.

In a new marriage real sexual trauma can occur when the couple is so emotionally insecure that they cannot deal with awkwardness and inexperience. Biological knowledge is essential, especially regarding the wife's somewhat more complex body and functioning. Husbands and wives both need to know that they have similar potentials for physical enjoyment. But more important is the larger knowledge that joy lies in their individual sense of self and their united ability to reinforce, reassure, and discover each other. Do they have sufficient patience and humor to enjoy teaching each other about their bodies and their emotions? Do they have the sense of identity which allows them to begin to become "one flesh" in their own unique way so that there eventually will be no distance between them? They learn to commune and unite in a special intimacy to which no one else is admitted. It is—or could be—theirs, exquisitely and exclusively. The supreme achievement of sexual unity is not orgasm, although this experience is often a special delight. Rather, it is the pristine realization that two souls, through passionate but disciplined preparation, are able to initiate each other into the rites of whole marital intimacy.

This is not to say that the orgasmic satisfaction of both partners is not important, especially for women. What portion of a female anatomy triggers the orgasmic response has been endlessly debated, remains debatable, and to a large extent is irrelevant. What *is* substantiated for most women is that a woman's climactic response to arousal occurs when it meets her personal requirements, among which are consideration, cleanliness, tenderness, and a feeling of being valued, being part of a committed relationship, as most clinicians have heard time and time again from women who feel emotionally exploited even when their husbands are technically skilled. In essence, she wants to be secure with an enduring, intimate relationship, and research reliably shows marital happiness is strongly correlated with sexual satisfaction.[2]

I regard with suspicion alleged recollections of how many minutes of arousal led to which frequencies and which levels of orgasm. If the experience is successful, it virtually excludes clinical introspection. Whether a couple achieves orgasm is important primarily if both husband and wife consider it important. How often and how intensely is also their private concern. Several friends, knowing of my professional efforts, have discreetly and appropriately related unmistakable information that orgasmic pleasure is real and regular in their own nurturant and intimate marriages. Further comment or inquiry would violate their privacy and mock the intention of this book. But those who doubt that physical joy is part of the total joy of secure, enduring marriages would profit from reading autobiographies and journals, looking for references to marital sexuality. One of the most intriguing is from the same Victoria whose name has become a synonym for prudery and sexual inhibition. She wrote of being "clasped and held tight in the sacred Hours at Night when the world seemed only to be ourselves." And, as a widow yearning for Albert, she mourned, "What a dreadful going to bed. *What* a contrast to that tender lover's love."[3]

Sexual Integrity

Proponents of premarital sexual activity argue that sex before commitment is a valid test of the future relationship. This is illogical in the extreme. There can be no valid test of the relationship without the weight of a very formal commitment. Those who claim that they have made a tentative commitment (as in the fad for "trial" marriages) are dealing in a contradiction of terms. Either the commitment is considered binding—in which case it amounts to something like marriage and might as well include the ceremony—or else it is a "yours-mine" contract with limitations, qualifications, and escape clauses.

Commitment is not possible without sexual integrity which avoids the extremes of aggressive sex on the one hand and sexual ignorance on the other. Sexual integrity acknowledges and celebrates one's own sexuality and that of one's partner, gives it an honored place in one's personality and behavior, but understands it to be only one element within a total personality.

Experience in counseling has taught me that one indicator of the person with sexual integrity is vocabulary. Such people have learned to speak of this important and private area of their lives in a vocabulary of gentle, warm, and respectful words, rather than the coldness of the clinic or the violent vulgarity of street terms. Another clue is that of healthy curiosity about sexual functioning that avoids the crudely experimental.

Furthermore, sexual integrity is highly correlated with premarital chastity and postmarital fidelity. This is only logical. Because erotic behaviors are so physically pleasurable, they can be powerfully distorting. Couples—whether married or unmarried—who see each other primarily as instruments of erotic gratification literally ignore personality and character while sensual pleasures dominate. Some people have affairs on that basis. Others, while remaining technically chaste—engaging in everything but full intercourse—are swept into marriage thinking to find relief from ungratified eroticism. Sexual compatibility is a very low common denominator indeed, and frequently weddings based upon this appetite are demeaning contracts, traditions which are a price that the man pays and that the woman exacts for gratification.

The much-decried but still firm connection between chastity and the ability to develop full intimacy and sexual compatibility after marriage flies in the face of much popular, though misguided, thinking about the role of religious teachings of sexuality.

Sexologists frequently assert that mankind's natural enjoyments have been warped by Judeo-Christian discomfort with the human body. They suggest that primitive tribes, before Western missionary influence, lived unclothed and uninhibited in their Edens. Simplistic reasoning like this almost always subjectively admires one trait and rejects another. By such reasoning, romanticists would envy the egalitarianism and carefree nakedness of the Yanomamo of Brazil and Venezuela. But do they envy these same people their unending warfare over sexual rights which results in nearly one-quarter of the men dying in battle?[4] There are impressive reasons for Judeo-Christian concern about the consequences of sexual behavior. Sexual intimacy is not a game to be played by children, and religious values adopted by believing people have been a way of giving them access to centuries of other people's experiences.

In several years of working with unwed parents, I have been frequently struck by their pathetic attempts to find identity through *doing* sex. Almost always it seemed that the boy-father was treated like a child by the girl-mother of his child. And the girl-mother saw the baby as inseparable from her own, always inadequate, identity. The most worrisome factor was the child's future with a mother—seldom with a father—who could not separate its identity from her own. These sad people desperately sought intimacy through sexual activity.

Chastity is not a refusal. It is an affirmation! It affirms, not denies, the value of sexuality and makes an honored place for intimacies within a value system. One wearies of silly dismissals of moral values by people who simply don't like the values they dismiss. These dismissals are intellectual temper tantrums.

However, we must take seriously the sincere and concerned people who suggest that religious traditions and rituals inhibit intimacy within marriage. Even though some people have used religious notions to justify prudishness and unhealthy mistrust of the body and its functions, anthropology is full of examples of societies which rely on ritual and tradition to give confidence in coping with life's demands. It is logical to expect that marriage, viewed and performed as a solemn ritual which must occur before sexual activity, will best free people to enjoy their intimate relationship. They are unburdened by guilt about violating either law or tradition. Indeed, if their values are Judeo-Christian, they believe they are authorized to "become one flesh" and enjoy each other with both mortal and divine approval. This would be no small factor in favor of chastity before and fidelity after the ritual of marriage. This is a hypothesis worth examining empirically.

Another logical but unstudied hypothesis—and one confirmed by people I have known through counseling and friendship—is that the couple who first experience premarital, nonsexual intimacy is much more likely to enjoy a full, whole, social, emotional and sexual life after marriage. And within marriage, problems such as premature ejaculation, vaginismus, and orgasmic inhibition are cured by intelligent and kindly relationships, supplemented by accurate biological understanding and, if needed, reliable professional assistance.

Consider the problem of premature ejaculation, which troubles many couples. The man's inability to defer his own climax is humiliating to him and frustrating to his wife. This problem is resolved rather rapidly and permanently within a mutually kind and supportive relationship by the wife caressing her husband as he guides her, telling her when to stop so that he learns to know his arousal pattern and can develop control over ejaculation. The technique is simple and applies to most sexual dysfunctions. Husband and wife must emotionally and physically *know* their bodies in ways other than full intercourse so that the intensity of intercourse becomes an extension of warm and nurturant caresses and not an act of aggression.

It is a sign of serious trouble when a couple physically enjoy each other only in total sexual intercourse. Many women suffer deeply in marriages in which they never know a caress, have their hand held warmly, or receive a tender embrace or a gentle kiss. More men than is commonly believed are troubled by the role society has imposed on them of being ever aroused, ever lustful. Along with the joys of total union, there are joys of quiet appreciation of one another, pleasurable but not crude, unembarrassed but not hedonistic. Perhaps the line is fine. Perhaps this is one more reason for privacy and integrity in intimacy, a justification for refusing to let outsiders dictate their version of "correct" sexual expression.

Loud proponents of irresponsible and exploitive sex have obscured the much quieter voices of those who prefer continence before and fidelity after marriage. A national survey of men and their sexual attitudes revealed that the majority of men base their marriage and their sexuality on love and companionship. Although not all demanded virginity before and fidelity after marriage, still many spoke strongly in favor of these values. One husband said that sexual intercourse before marriage was wrong and that after marriage "you can learn together—it really doesn't require experience. . . . Any normal human would have romantic encounters, but I would prefer that it not include intercourse."[5] Another husband said: "I wanted a virgin wife. Both I and my wife were virgins. P.S. Our sex life in marriage has been *extremely* fulfilling, exciting and adventurous."[6]

In another study of a hundred thousand women, the preference for marital commitment before sexual involvement was expressed more often than not, a preference all the more striking when we remember that much premarital sexual intercourse, perhaps most, occurs between people who intend to marry each other.[7] One woman expressed her views about premarital sexuality: "Monogamy and fidelity are for me the way to happiness. If a couple has love, trust and mutual respect for each other, experimenting beforehand is not necessary. Their sex lives will work out naturally."[8]

The questions the couple must answer before marriage concern not their erotic skills but their capacity to be secure, kindly, and respectful of each other. Is their relationship benevolent and likely to enhance each other? If these concerns are tested and answered before marriage without the distraction of sex, the couple can anticipate full sexual enjoyment. But if they reverse this process, the chances are high that sex will be unable to outweigh the detriments of social and emotional incompatibility. In the woman's study were found correlations between premarital sexual activity, a low level of education, and personal unhappiness.[9] This is but one example of how, time and again, our society mistakes sexual familiarity for sexual knowledge.

For example, some recent experiments suggest that men and women are potentially quite similar in sexual arousal and response. Both can be "turned on" rapidly, and both can learn to be excited by pornography or exploitive sex. Such experiments neglect to ask whether such behavior is either desirable or helpful in an intimate relationship for either women or men. The biological fact that women can be sexually abrupt does not answer the question of whether the gentle arousal of caresses, conversation, and tenderness might add a psychological dimension of pleasure valuable for its own sake to both people. There are realities besides biological capacity. Some of them may be indescribable and probably should remain so.

I counseled with one couple who were dissatisfied with their sexual compatibility. The wife was offended by her husband's use of pornography in his attempts to arouse her, preferring his kindness and respect to the technical contortions he found exciting. It was clear that the communication gap was severe when the husband urged her to learn to appreciate his pornography *"like a man."*

This case, though extreme, indicates a common problem in most marriages. Husbands and wives come to the marital "union" far from united and must work at achieving it. The newly available information about biological functioning, though it must be used carefully, is helpful in establishing the fact that the biological causes for different sexual responses between men and women are fewer than has been popularly imagined. That means most differences are culturally imposed or are personal. It should be reassuring to couples to realize that what they perceived as fixed limitations may be only assumptions that they accepted too quickly.

For example, young couples typically play stereotyped roles. He is aggressive—at work, at play, at sex. She is somewhat more passive and dependent. Many young couples cling to these roles out of insecurity and ignorance in how to establish new ones. In extreme cases, particularly if the wife's experiences before marriage left her identity insecure, she may accept her husband's insensitivity without resistance, even when it involves exploitation and abuse. Frequently, in such sad, sick situations, both husband and wife have seen similar patterns with their parents and grandparents. Both may feel that this is the way men treat women and cannot imagine a benevolent relationship. Lacking the skills to negotiate a more equitable relationship, they can almost never change their relationship without help. And obviously, until even healthy couples find a way to break out of stereotyped reactions to each other, their search for full intimacy is hampered.

In normal marriages, however, time and circumstances take over. The realities of motherhood comprehensively strengthen a passive bride's integrity, powerfully refining her identity, role, and skills. She doesn't really have to ask herself if she is important in anyone's scheme of things. The husband, in the first decade or so, is usually caught up in his vocation, trapped by his own cultural messages that he can wait until his children are teenagers or that he should concentrate on breadwinning rather than on nurturance. However, during the thirties or forties, reality also begins teaching him. As one man put it, "I began to realize I would never win the Nobel Prize." The body weakens slightly but perceptibly. Younger men become supervisors at work. And he discovers his own need to nurture. He experiences the emotional and social transition known as the midlife crisis.

If the marriage partners have a healthy relationship and are committed to each other, it can be an exciting time of growth for both. Unfortunately, many marriages break up during this period if either partner is frightened by the change, resents it, or —blindly—blames the spouse for all those "old" problems. If the couple chooses to grow closer, these social and emotional changes can be reflected in their sexual life. The husband can desire and experience the communion and union of intimacy as never before. He can divest himself of the stereotyped exploitations and aggression he practiced earlier. The wife's new self-certitude enables her to enjoy her own desires and in her own way be free of detrimental stereotypes. As they both rediscover themselves, though they may have started out with drastically different conceptions of sexuality, identity, and intimacy, they are now able to achieve new unity. They reject stereotypes about each other and acquire new respect for each other. As he enjoys her new strengths, she enjoys his new tenderness. Both benefit from modifying their own former expectations. In other words, love in each succeeding decade of marriage can be better than ever before, contrary to every TV formula.

Warren and Wilma made such a discovery. They had engaged in premarital sexual activity but Wilma was confused to find that she both enjoyed physical relations and felt guilty for violating her moral code. Warren disregarded her guilt, especially after marriage, and expected her to enter into more extravagant sexual explorations. After several years, they turned to technique books for more ideas or erotic methods but still found their excitement diminishing. They were considering divorce when the idea occurred to them that their expectations were unrealistic. As they came to understand each other better and appreciated that they were maturing in spirit as well as body, Wilma and Warren began to redefine intimacy. As a result, they rejected much of their past and concentrated on each other as whole companions rather than sexual partners. As they became gentler, their passion increased because it now included their whole relationship, not just a physical fragment.

Reality does not permit us to indulge in the hope that all young men are or will become sensitive to the needs of their young wives and that all young women will enter marriage as whole and self-respecting individuals. Even so, no matter what age we might be, we need to learn that sexual integrity is part of the foundation of an ever-deepening intimacy—a union of hopes, feelings, and experiences so profound that joyous physical union is its symbol in enduring marriages.

Enduring Marriage

We are force-fed emotions even while we passively watch television in our homes. Very young writers, semi-young directors, and imitation-young actors all assure us that we must live "with gusto." Weary and financially battered, we seldom do the things those unmarried (or semi-married) people do in their childless, new-car world. Nevertheless it registers, and we perceive our ordinary lives as bland in comparison to the screen portrayal of virility, materialism, variety, and escape. Children, bills, and employment never hinder television folk in their pursuit of pleasure. Successful people and their "liberated" sexual partners have money, new cars, decorator-furnished apartments, and endless physical energy for touch football and seduction. We despair as we compare ourselves unfavorably to the gusto life. Our marriages seem especially dull compared to their glamorous succession of love affairs.

In real marriages, after the first few weeks, months, or years, longer-range realities intrude. The novelty is gone. But if the foundation of a marriage is broad and deep, sexual enjoyments can enter their most refined and richest phase in these later years, because, through enduring, the husband and wife have achieved a deeper level of intimacy. In one study, a woman succinctly placed sexuality within its proper context of the whole relationship: "A happy, sexually fulfilled woman is a woman who is able to communicate with her husband. After 33 years of marriage I know that women require intimacy, the intimacy that leads to free expression. Too many men refuse to recognize this. Trouble in marriage comes from the refusal to recognize that partners grow and change over the years, from the lack of communication about emotional needs as well as physical ones."[10] The couple has, at this point, *achieved* union, a steadier, more contented bulwark against life stresses, a kind of equilibrium that enables them to absorb, face, and solve problems with increasing efficiency as they move through the years.[11] One of those stresses can be the changing nature of the sexual relationship itself, but the solution is its own reward, as strongly committed married couples know.

All too often, however, we ignore the fact that a process is governed by its own laws. More than one friend and client has announced the decision to seek a divorce and when asked "Why?" has responded, "Because she (or he) doesn't turn me on." This rejects reality. In the case of one woman it was real that her husband earned an excellent income, loved their children, was faithful to her, and was apparently emotionally bland. It was also real that their children were very active and close in age, that the house was always untidy, and that expenses exceeded income. It was an illusion that there was someone waiting for her who would love her children, earn an even more excellent income, be faithful, and "turn her on" by his charm. She did not understand that a relationship becomes satisfying when it is nurtured, and instead demanded satisfaction before she was willing to work on it. Furthermore, she had accepted the illusion that we can successfully remove intimacy from the structure of marriage and family. In reality, intimacy must include an active commitment to those we claim to love. And to endure, intimacy must be part of an ongoing structure. Breaking through the barrier that guards close relationships takes major effort and energy. It is at once a simple yet difficult experience. It is partially based on the sheer duration of years together. Even more important is a respect for the partner's personality coupled with an intense personal devotion to the marriage, a commitment of character.

Deep marital companionships include common and uncommon courtesies, apologies, ministering to an ill spouse, sharing sunsets, and weeding the garden. Over time we learn to understand or at least tolerate the dark moods of the other and to redirect our own. We quietly exult in the success of our companion whether it be a successful monthly checkbook balance or a major civic volunteer task well done. Hurt by criticism, we lash out, later to reconcile in tears for verbally assaulting this most precious life which we share. We keep the difficult world at bay for a while as we embrace in the sanctity of our own private, mutually honored bed. This sanctity is exquisite and beyond description. It is not portrayed by the media because it cannot be, but it is instead routinely mocked by the formula dramas that show a long-term marriage as dull and self-destroying, needing a little infidelity to either spice up the marriage itself or reaffirm the adulterer's worth. It is disconcerting to consider that marital hypocrisy has become an expected element in emotional success. What is dismaying is the popular impression given that adultery, cruelty, promise-breaking, and irresponsibility have no negative consequences.

Such moral shallowness would be indecent enough if the audience consisted of jaded and cynical people. That a good share of the audience are lonely and vulnerable people seeking relief from the pain of emotional isolation makes such "entertainment" repellently exploitive.

Confronted with this debased and debasing emphasis on sex, without integrity, it is reassuring to find instances of real people affirming real values by their behavior. When author Cornelius Ryan's radiation treatment therapy for cancer of the prostate resulted in sterility and probable impotence, Kathryn Morgan Ryan placed sex in the context of their enduring companionship:

> He did not know if I could accept the possibility of his celibacy. The absence of sexual relationships, if it became total, might, he felt, prove difficult for me to cope with. In the strangest conversation we had ever had, Connie at one point said, "I could never blame you if you did something about it. Just don't ever let me know."
>
> . . . I explained my feelings to him as best I could. I had not expected that sexual functions could ever again be the same as in the past, nor had they been during the year of worry and concern about Connie's health. . . . I had become reconciled to the gradual phasing-out of the sexual aspect of our lives. What had once been an important part of our marriage had diminished, and I told Connie that, among my priorities, sex had no listing. If it occurred, if it *could* occur, it would be a bonus, treasured and enjoyed all the more for its rarity.
>
> At that time I was still in my early forties. Admittedly, I have given the subject private thought. Any woman would have done so. But my admiration and regard for Connie were strong aspects of our marriage. I was proud of my husband and proud to be his

> wife. . . . I could not see myself seeking temporary liaisons, much less living with the guilt that would have followed. An unfaithful act by me, no matter how discreet, would have smudged and tainted all that we had found together.
>
> Yet, there was a moment when the temptation was strong. My physical desires were unchanged even as Connie's were waning. It would have been easy to satisfy them. I think what held me back most were certain facets of my husband's personality that were highly meaningful to me: his code of honor and ethics, his passion for truth, his sense of self. Had our roles been reversed I think Connie would have remained faithful to me. The rules of conduct by which he lived were deeply ingrained, and he would have adhered to them. I think, too, that my marriage vows, as well as the traits I admired in Connie, kept me from engaging in extramarital sex. I had promised to love and cherish him in *sickness* and in health, clinging only unto him. It is a rather simplistic and possibly old-fashioned philosophy . . . I think I loved my husband in his years of sickness more than at any time in our marriage, and the way he handled his illness, the fierce courage with which he fought it, submerged my sexual desires as my pride in him increased. I cherished him too much to be unfaithful to him.
>
> I have mentioned this because other women, younger women, could well have considered the time ahead as barren, the gift and joy of mating too great a treasure to live without. I sympathize strongly with that concept. No one has said it is easy to abstain from sexual pleasure.[12]

My clinical experience provides similar insights about the place of sex in the total relationship from a much younger marriage. After five years of marriage, Martin had developed an affectionate, though not adulterous, relationship with a woman at work. When Esther discovered a love letter and confronted him, he affirmed his interest in the other woman and moved out of the home. Their clergyman intervened; and because of feelings for his two children, Martin moved back in, declaring that he had no feelings for his wife. They sought counseling.

In that process, I learned that sexual intercourse had begun many months before their marriage. Esther reported that their wedding night had been "just more of the same." Their physical interest in each other waned in competition with school, work, children, and the usual challenges and distractions of young marrieds until, when the separation came, they had not engaged in sexual intercourse for several months. However, the therapy focused on the problems they defined as particularly crucial—finances and children's anxieties. After we had been working together about four months, Esther reported that some well-meaning friends and relatives, knowing that over a year had passed without sexual relations, were urging her to "give Martin what every man has to have."

This outside interference was very misguided. Esther and Martin's values system emphasized premarital chastity. Both people, especially Esther, expressed severe guilt about their premarital behavior. They had decided to honor their values and, though married, not return to sexual activity until trust, security, and respect had been restored, along with a commitment to stay married.* They recognized that their sexual activity had distracted them from getting to know each other's personality and character before marriage and, in essence, had decided now to do what they should have done before marrying.

Several weeks passed, and then Esther called to report that they had considered resuming sexual activity but felt awkward. After discussion, she recognized that this was to be expected as she and Martin rediscovered each other. Later, another question had to do with shyness about undressing in the same room again, a routine procedure during their time of estrangement and hostility. Now that they were trying to develop self-esteem and mutual respect, their bodies were assuming new meaning—not shame but rather new importance. After a two-week silence, Esther reported: "We resumed our relations. I never dreamed it

---

* It remains a source of wonder that many therapists seek to deal with guilt by denouncing all guilt-producing values. Such total interference with client value systems requires virtual infallibility, for the therapist would have to know precisely which values he could safely undermine and which are necessary for the client's mental well-being and social stability.

could be like that. It was so special that I really would rather not talk about it." And she didn't.

Now, after several years, this couple is achieving a steady, strong intimacy. Martin is more outgoing, Esther is obviously quieter, yet neither has abandoned basic identity. He enjoys her quietness and she appreciates his spontaneity. Martin's role as an active husband and father is clearer. Esther's role as an active wife and mother is also clearer. Both complement each other as homebuilders. Their outward appearance is that of two devoted companions, neither naive nor burdened. Occasional visits elicit the report that their intimacy deepens and new joys are experienced.

Is all well? No. Their finances are disastrous, which creates much strain. Esther tends to oscillate between contentment and despair. Are they succeeding? Yes. They are more intimate by far, they are working together, and life has deeper, more rewarding significance.

Sexuality and Procreation

Those who feel that erotic climax is the ultimate sexual experience have bought one of the shabbiest illusions of our culture. When we embrace either in creative union or in symbolism of it, we expand our sexuality far beyond mere pleasure.

First, we exercise profound power as life is created by the literal union of our seed. Second, by nurturing that life to become a human being, we relive and reorder our own lives. Third, by creating and nurturing life we begin to find our place in the human family and our particular part of it.

These three facets of procreation give us place — identity — in history. They bind humanity together. No one who has nurtured his own child can look upon his fellow humans without increased compassion.

To be sure, sexual intimacy occurs most of the time without pregnancy resulting. For those who desire to create life and nurture it (and nurturing can follow either procreation or adoption), sexual union becomes an intimate communion and reunion which symbolically reaffirms their intimacy and commitment. It could even be called a rite of enduring marriage.

Children add stress to marriage but this stress with its potentially unlimited rewards must be compared to life's other inevitable stresses in a voluntarily childless marriage which has no such rewards.

Conclusion

What, then, is benevolent, enduring marriage? I believe it is the union of two clear identities which intensifies and enhances each. Marriage companions learn and refine new roles, developing the relationship skills of total union.

The companionship of enduring marriage is both a rationale and a reward for living, answering our deep need for intimacy. This companion is a unique friend with whom to battle the dragons of life and savor the nectars of victory.

Some people find such a long-term commitment boring. Others fear that it will be too demanding. If it is healthy, its giving, sharing, and investing generate new energies, restoring even though it taxes to the utmost.

It is never too late to begin the quest for committed intimacy if both partners are willing. Unparalleled flexibility is the blessing and trial of being human. The traumatized child can find a benevolent world later. The lonely adolescent can become a secure and gregarious adult. Many couples lustfully stumble into marriage, have horrendous honeymoons, exploit each other during the first years, yet eventually develop a benevolent intimacy.

An exceptionally rewarding experience occurred one evening at a church social. As a certain couple arrived, a friend commented that he liked their example of mutual affection. "In fact," he said, "they inspire me to continually improve my marriage." I agreed. The couple held hands almost continuously, not conspicuously but in a natural coming together. They spoke to the many people who walked over to greet them, for they were well liked, but in between they obviously enjoyed being together. I knew this couple well for I had been part of their marriage counseling at a time when their troubles had been severe enough to consider divorce. Once I had helped them. Now I found myself learning from their intimacy, as I have from all those who have shared their experiences with me. It is the consequences of the remarkable yet ordinary lives of these people which support the ideas offered in this book. Through them I know that within the loyal embraces of those who endure, true intimacy with full sexuality flourishes.

AFTERWORD

Statistics indicate that over 90 percent of American adults marry. The great majority who lose a spouse through death or divorce also remarry, and most of those who live together without marriage intend to marry. Despite all of the fuss and frenzy about the endangered family, it remains the most common human structure in our society.

What is in danger is the emotional fabric of the family, and hence the emotional fabric of our society. There is no other universal source of emotional strength that even slightly approximates the family; thus, our concern cannot be misplaced. For better or worse, we learn identity in our families. Family interactions teach us our roles. Within the family we rehearse our relationship skills. And no physical or emotional activity—not work, recreation, congregational worship, nor education—offers the potential for intimacy that the family does.

Unquestionably, today's family is fragile. The fact that marriages and families break up more frequently these days does not eliminate their social and emotional benefits—or console those who must deal with the void of such loss. One eloquent record was left in *Haywire,* the autobiography of Brooke Hayward. Raised in wealth and fame, by twenty-three she had also dealt with the suicides of her famous actress-mother and her withdrawn sister, the insanity of her brother, and the lingering death of her well-known and well-to-do father. Her father had married five times, her mother four. Brooke herself is divorced with three children. In her father's hospital room, she holds his lifeless body and weeps:

> I wept for my family, all of us, my beautiful, idyllic, lost family. I wept for our excesses, our delusions and inconsistencies; not that we had cared too much or too little, although both were true, but that we had let such extraordinary care be subverted into such extraordinary carelessness. We'd been careless with the best of our many resources: each other. It was as if we'd taken for granted the

> fact that, like our talents and interests, and riches, there would be more where *we* had come from, too; another chance, another summer, another Brooke or Bridget or Bill.[1]

According to the thesis of this book, some things do not change or they change very little. A human being in the year 900, 1900, or 1990 needs to develop a sense of identity, effective roles, and rewarding relationship skills or he or she cannot enjoy the intimacy that makes us fully human. This is seldom understood by many social forecasters, who are not particularly optimistic about our future due to technological problems, nuclear war, economic disintegration, and crippling energy shortages that will reverse the basis of our life-style. This very preoccupation with technology insidiously wears away our capacity to achieve human intimacy. Ethically, it manifests itself as materialism. Socially and emotionally it manifests itself as functionalism divorced from human values.

It is all too human to take comfort from things rather than people. The ability to procure and flaunt expensive toys is as characteristic of some adults as it is of some children. Someone insecure in identity takes ego comfort from having a prestigious university's diploma, applause at a professional conference, or acceptance by an exclusive country club. Many husbands and fathers—and increasing numbers of wives and mothers—make civic, church, and professional reputations for effective and creative work. Yet far too many of these same "achieving" people feel uncomfortable and unable to respond adequately when a spouse says, "I'm lonely," or a child says, "I need to talk."

Social and emotional closeness is not amenable to management by objectives and does not work smoothly into flow charts. It does not follow schedules. It makes inordinate demands and makes them at inconvenient times. Frequently the problem is much clearer than the solution and even well-meaning efforts may have apparently disastrous results. And sometimes rewards are delayed for years. (I believe that grandparents enjoy their grandchildren so much because their spontaneous affection, energy, and wonder come as a reward, outweighing responsibility, after years of giving.)

A technological emphasis in one's life has none of these disadvantages. It offers specific formulas, clear rewards for clearly defined duties, and precise evaluations. But it cannot offer intimacy. Ask any retired person who visited his former workplace. Technology defines progress as "newer" and satisfaction as "efficiency." Dolby Stereo is not a musical advance, merely an electronic innovation. For the greatest adventure of our generation, man's landing on the moon, astronauts were chosen who could be interchangeable parts of a technological network of rockets, computers, and machines. *Star Wars,* that special-effects entertainment tour de force, has machines that are almost human (R2D2) and humans that are almost machines (Darth Vader). Owning a Mercedes says nothing about the quality of the owner's mind and heart.

Our preoccupation with technical novelty extends to human behavior as well. This year some seek spiritual solace in hot-tub encounter groups while others seek gratification in sex-and-pain establishments. Last year it was other fads. Next year it will be still others. By comparison, a steady job, the same spouse, and getting the children's teeth straightened seem like the quintessence of drudgery. There are even active churchgoers who equate material success with their worth as a human being.

It has never been more crucial to sort illusions from reality. I believe that unless we look ahead, we will face even worse dangers from our technological illusions. Things cannot nurture the human spirit. And if the spirit goes unnurtured, within a few short years it will become inhumane. This is the morbid lesson of Nazi Germany and Stalinist Russia. It is also the lesson our children unknowingly teach every time they say, "I'm bored." Surrounded by things, they do not enjoy being alive.

There is grave cause for concern but not necessarily pessimism. The hunger for intimacy is, next to survival needs, our deepest human longing. The very bizarreness of the searches we see today testifies to the strength of that hunger. And people who have once tasted bread will not willingly return to stones.

Recently a couple came in for counseling. They were feeling severe financial stress but even more emotional distress because two of their three children were exhibiting mental and sexual disturbances. Together we examined the components of their life: their schedule, their obligations outside the home, the quality of relationships within the home. They shared their perception of their identities, defined their roles, analyzed their relationship skills. That process focused some issues for them clearly and they found themselves returning again and again to the diagnosis that everyone in the family, themselves included, was starving for intimacy. They rearranged their priorities immediately and within two weeks the climate of the home had begun to change. They were emotionally available to their children and to each other. They reported new tenderness in their family. Five deprived human beings were reviving from infusions of intimacy.

To this couple sexuality is special, symbolically and literally reaffirming their commitment as they embrace in total union. Yet it is only a part. Their hungers were not filled alone by their private intimacy. They saw and responded to the needs of their children, and their children responded to *their* needs. And they reached out to their extended family and friends.

With virtually unlimited technology and material comfort at our disposal, we fluctuate between superficial involvements and find them empty of fulfillment. The ancient reality remains: with integrity and discipline we can attain most, perhaps all, of life's true pleasure and true security by learning to talk with, touch, and in other ways enjoy true intimacy with each other.

NOTES

Chapter One
The Illusions and Realities of Human Intimacy

1. C. S. Lewis, *The Screwtape Letters* and *Screwtape Proposes a Toast* (New York: The Macmillan Company/Paperbacks edition, 1971), pp. 142-44.

2. George F. Will, "A Right to Health," *Newsweek*, 7 August 1978, p. 88.

3. James E. Enstrom, "CA/A Cancer Journal for Clinicians," *American Cancer Society* 29 (November-December 1979): 352-61.

4. See the general discussion in Nicholas A. Groth, *Men Who Rape* (New York: Plenum Press, 1979).

5. Don Ateyo, *Blood and Guts: Violence in Sports* (London: Paddington Press Ltd., 1979), pp. 220-21.

6. Mavis E. Hetherington, "Divorce, A Child's Perspective," *American Psychologist* 34 (October 1979): 857.

7. Judith S. Wallerstein and Joan B. Kelly, "California's Children of Divorce," *Psychology Today* 13 (January 1980): 68.

8. Lee Salk, *What Every Child Would Like Parents to Know about Divorce* (New York: Harper and Row Publishers, 1978), pp. 1-2.

9. William H. Masters and Virginia E. Johnson, *The Pleasure Bond* (New York: Bantam Books, 1974), pp. 155, 185.

10. National Geographic Society, *Energy: A Special Report* (Washington, D.C.: National Geographic Society, 1981), p. 22.

11. Helen Singer Kaplan, *The New Sex Therapy* (New York: Brunner/Mazel, 1974), p. 110.

12. William H. Masters and Virginia E. Johnson, *Homosexuality in Perspective* (Boston: Little, Brown and Co., 1979), pp. 222-23.

13. *Ibid.*, p. 173.

14. Helen Singer Kaplan, *Disorders of Sexual Desire* (New York: Brunner/Mazel, 1979), p. 58.

15. As cited in James J. Lynch, *The Broken Heart: The Medical Consequences of Loneliness* (New York: Basic Books, Inc., 1977), pp. 21-35.

16. Harry C. Merserve, "Forever," *Journal of Religion and Health* 16, no. 4 (1977): 251-54.

17. Peter Drucker, "What Freud Forgot," *Human Nature* 2 (March 1979): 44. See also Drucker, *Adventures of a Bystander* (New York: Harper and Row Publishers, 1978).

18. Frank J. Sulloway, *Freud: Biologist of the Mind* (New York: Basic Books, 1979), p. 499.

19. Will Durant and Ariel Durant, *Rousseau and Revolution,* vol. 10 in *The Story of Civilization* (New York: Simon and Schuster, 1967), p. 886.

20. Lee M. Hollander, ed. and trans., *Selections from the Writings of Kierkegaard* (Garden City, NY: Doubleday and Company, Inc., 1960), pp. 10-11.

21. Janko Larrin, *Nietzsche: A Biographical Introduction* (New York: Charles Scribner's Sons, 1971), pp. 104, 171.

22. Lynch, *The Broken Heart,* p. 13.

23. Barton E. Bernstein, "Legal and Social Interface in Counseling Homosexual Clients," *Social Casework* 58 (January 1977): 36, 39-40.

24. Alan P. Bell and Martin S. Weinberg, *Homosexualities: A Study of Diversities among Men and Women* (New York: Simon and Schuster, 1978), pp. 175, 199.

25. Karen Kenyon, "A Survivor's Notes," *Newsweek,* 30 April 1979, p. 17.

26. "On the Conflicts between Biological and Social Evolution and between Psychology and Moral Tradition," *American Psychologist* 30 (December 1975): 1120-21.

27. Viktor Frankl, *Man's Search for Meaning* (New York: Pocket Books, 1963), pp. 57-61.

Chapter Two
The Reality of Identity

1. Burton L. White, *The First Three Years of Life* (Englewood Cliffs: Prentice-Hall, 1975), p. 255.

2. Erich Fromm, *The Heart of Man: Its Genius for Good and Evil* (New York: Harper and Row, 1964), pp. 28-29.

3. Arthur Henly, *Demon in My View* (New York: Trident Press, 1966), pp. 1-7.

4. Bruno Bettelheim, *The Uses of Enchantment* (New York: Vintage Books, 1977), p. 9.

5. Arlene Skolnick, "The Myth of the Vulnerable Child," *Psychology Today* 11 (February 1978): 56-58, 60-65.

6. Benjamin De Mott, "The Pro-Incest Lobby," *Psychology Today* 13 (March 1980): 15-16. For an extended study see Karin C. Meiselman, *Incest* (San Francisco: Jossey-Bass Publishers, 1978).

7. White, *The First Three Years,* p. 264.

Chapter Three
The Illusion of Stereotypes
The Reality of Roles

1. William Foote Whyte, *Street Corner Society* (Chicago: University of Chicago Press, 1955). See also Denise B. Kandel, "Homophyly, Selections and Socialization in Adolescents," *American Journal of Sociology* 84 (September 1978): 427-36.

2. Jon K. Meyer and Donna J. Reter, "Sex Reassignment: Follow-up," *Archives of General Psychiatry* 36 (August 1979): 1014.

3. C. S. Lewis, *A Grief Observed* (New York: Bantam Books, Inc., 1976), pp. 57-58.

4. Sandra L. Bem, "The Measurement of Psychological Androgyny," *Journal of Consulting and Clinical Psychology* 42, no. 2 (1974): 156.

5. Ivan Boszormenyi-Nagy and Geraldine M. Spark, *Invisible Loyalties* (Hagerstown, MD: Harper and Row Publishers, Inc., 1973), p. 12.

6. "A Biosocial Perspective on Parentage," *Daedalus* 106 (Spring 1977): 1-31.

7. Perhaps the most useful summary available on research about fathering is Michael E. Lamb, *The Role of the Father in Child Development* (New York: John Wiley & Sons, 1976).

8. Melford Spiro, *Gender and Culture: Kibbutz Women Revisited* (Durham, ND: Duke University Press, 1979), pp. 6, 14, 25-29, 32-33, 36, 42, 109-110. See also Benjamin Beit-Hallahmi and Albert I. Rabin, "The Kibbutz as a Social Experiment and as a Child-Rearing Laboratory," *American Psychologist* 32, no. 7 (1977): 532-41.

9. Spiro, *Gender and Culture*, pp. 37-38.

10. "The Nation's New Schoolmistress," *Newsweek*, 12 November 1979, p. 41.

11. Bea Pixa, "Talking to Women about the Rest of Their Lives," *San Francisco Sunday Examiner & Chronicle*, 30 September 1979, p. 5.

12. Dorothy Rogers, *The Adult Years: An Introduction to Aging* (Englewood Cliffs, NJ: Prentice-Hall, Inc., 1979), p. 100.

13. William Miller, as told to Frances S. Leighton, *Fishbait* (Englewood Cliffs, NJ: Prentice-Hall, Inc., 1977), pp. 79-80.

14. George A. Rekers, "Atypical Gender Development and Psychosocial Adjustment," *Journal of Applied Behavior Analysis* 10 (1977): 556.

Chapter Four
The Illusion of Sexual Exploitation
The Reality of Relationship Skills

1. Lenore Tiefer, "The Kiss," *Human Nature* 1 (July 1978): 28-37.

2. Kenneth L. Cannon, *Developing a Marriage Relationship* (Provo, UT: Brigham Young University Press, 1972), p. 17. See the widely quoted M. I. Saghir and E. Robins, *Male and Female Homosexuality* (Baltimore: The Williams and Wilkins Company, 1973), pp. 36-37 for an example of confusing eroticism with relationship skills.

3. James J. Lynch, *The Broken Heart: The Medical Consequences of Loneliness* (New York: Basic Books, Inc., 1977), p. 101.

4. Corrie ten Boom, *Prison Letters* (New York: Bantam Books, Inc., 1975), p. 47, is one example.

5. Alfred Charles Kinsey, Wardell B. Pomeroy and Clyde E. Martin, *Sexual Behavior in the Human Male* (Philadelphia: W. B. Saunders Company, 1948), p. 498.

6. Albert Bandura, "The Stormy Decade: Fact or Fiction," *Psychology in the Schools* 1 (July 1964): 224-31.

7. Helen Singer Kaplan, *The New Sex Therapy* (New York: Brunner/Mazel, 1974), pp. 145-146.

8. Jonathan L. Freedman, *Introductory Psychology* (Reading, MA: Addison-Wesley Publishing Company, Inc., 1978), glossary, p. A37.

9. Alfred Freedman, Harold I. Kaplan, and Benjamin J. Sadocks, eds., *Comprehensive Textbook of Psychiatry*, 2 vols. (Baltimore: The Williams and Wilkins Company, 1975), 2: 2583.

10. Abraham H. Maslow, *Motivation and Personality* (New York: Harper and Row Publishers, 1954), pp. 20-21.

11. Kenneth B. Hardy, "An Appetitional Theory of Sexual Motivation," *Psychological Review* 71, no. 1 (1964): 1-18.

12. John Bancroft, "The Relationship between Hormones and Sexual Behavior in Humans," *Biological Determinants of Sexual Behavior*, ed. J. B. Hutchinson (New York: John Wiley and Sons, 1978), p. 493.

13. S. L. Washburn, "What We Can't Learn about People from Apes," *Human Nature*, November 1978, p. 70.

14. Robert Meyers, "A Couple That Could," *Psychology Today* 12 (November 1978): 107.

15. William H. Masters and Virginia E. Johnson, *The Pleasure Bond* (New York: Bantam Books, 1974), p. 3.

16. *Ibid.*

17. C. S. Lewis, *The Allegory of Love* (London: Oxford University Press, 1936), p. 196.

18. Seymour Feshback and Neal Malamuth, "Sex and Aggression: Proving the Link," *Psychology Today* 12 (November 1978): 114, 117, 122.

19. To see this pattern it is helpful to review all the case excerpts throughout William H. Masters and Virginia E. Johnson, *Homosexuality in Perspective* (Boston: Little, Brown and Company, 1979).

20. Helen Singer Kaplan, *Disorders of Sexual Desires* (New York: Brunner/Mazel, 1979), p. 94.

21. The virtue of masturbation is the overall theme of Susanne Sarnoff and Irving Sarnoff, *Sexual Excitement, Sexual Peace* (New York: M. Evans and Company, Inc., 1979).

22. *Ibid.*, p. 1.

23. Kinsey, Pomeroy, and Martin, *Sexual Behavior*, pp. 238-239.

24. *Ibid.*, p. 238.

25. *Ibid.*, pp. 240-241.

26. Sarnoff and Sarnoff, *Sexual Excitement*, p. 28.

27. R. J. McGuire, J. M. Carlisle, B. G. Young, "Sexual Deviations as Conditioned Behavior: A Hypothesis," *Behavior Research and Therapy* 2 (1965): 185.

28. Gerald C. Davison, "Elimination of a Sadistic Fantasy by a Client-Controlled Counterconditioning Technique," *Journal of Abnormal Psychology* 73, no. 1 (1968): 84-90.

29. Sarnoff and Sarnoff, *Sexual Excitement*, p. 28.

30. Disturbed by this growing trend, one psychotherapist devised an effective means of teaching self-control. See Allen E. Bergin, "A Self-Regulation Technique for Impulse Control Disorders," *Psychotherapy: Theory, Research and Practice* 6 (1969): 113-18.

31. See Charles E. Moan and Robert G. Heath, "Septal Stimulation for the Initiation of Heterosexual Behavior in a Homosexual Male," *Journal of Behavior Therapy and Experimental Psychiatry* 3 (1972): 23-30, for a report of such therapy.

32. Alice S. Rossi, "Maternalism, Sexuality, and the New Feminism," in Joseph Zubin and John Money, eds., *Contemporary Sexual Behavior* (Baltimore: Johns Hopkins University Press, 1973), p. 159.

Chapter Five
Beginning Marriage: The Illusion of Cohabitation The Reality of Homebuilding

1. C. P. Kottak, *Anthropology: The Exploration of Human Diversity* (New York: Random House, 1974), p. 285.

2. Azubike Felix Uzoka, "The Myth of the Nuclear Family," *American Psychologist,* November 1979, pp. 1095-1106.

3. Carol Tavris and Susan Sadd, *The Redbook Report on Female Sexuality* (New York: The Delacorte Press, 1977), pp. 12-23.

4. William J. Lederer and Don D. Jackson, *The Mirages of Marriage* (New York: W. W. Norton and Company, 1968), p. 135.

5. *Ibid.*, p. 130.

6. Lewis A. Coser, *The Functions of Social Conflict* (Glencoe, IL: The Free Press, 1956).

7. James J. Lynch, *The Broken Heart: The Medical Consequences of Loneliness* (New York: Basic Books, Inc., 1977), p. 3.

8. Arno Karlen, *Sexuality and Homosexuality* (New York: W. W. Norton and Company, Inc., 1971), pp. 47-48.

9. Neil Gilbert, "An Initial Agenda for Family Policy," *Social Work* 24, no. 6 (1979): 448.

10. Lynch, *Broken Heart,* pp. 34-35, 47-49, 53, 58, 240-41.

11. As cited in Lynch, *Broken Heart,* p. 7.

12. Dorothy Rogers, *The Adult Years: An Introduction to Aging* (Englewood Cliffs, NJ: Prentice Hall, Inc., 1979), p. 97.

13. Urie Bronfenbrenner, "Context of Child Rearing: Problems and Prospects," *American Psychologist* 34 (October 1979): 844.

14. Dolores Gold and David Andres, "Developmental Comparisons between Ten-Year-Old Children with Employed and Non-employed Mothers," *Child Development* 49, no. 1 (March 1978): 83.

15. Sheldon Vanauken, *A Severe Mercy* (San Francisco: Harper and Row Publishers, 1977), p. 209.

16. Lois W. Hoffman, "Maternal Employment: 1979," *American Psychologist* 24 (October 1979): 860.

17. Scott Lloyd, "Is the Woman's Place Really in the Home?" *BYU Today* 3 (December 1979): 11-12.

18. *Ibid.*

19. U.S. Bureau of the Census, *Statistical Abstract of the U.S.: 1978* (99th ed.), Washington, D.C., 1978.

20. George C. Homans, *The Human Group* (New York: Harcourt, Brace, and World, Inc., 1950), pp. 48-50.

21. See, for example, Karen Schaar, "Vermont: Getting Through the Adult Years," *APA Monitor* (September-October 1978), p. 29; Robert R. Sears, "Sources of Life Satisfactions of the Terman Gifted Men," *American Psychologist* 32, no. 2 (1977): 119-28; and Mihaly Csikszentmihalyi and Ronald Graef, "Feeling Free," *Psychology Today* 13 (December 1979): 84-99.

22. Louis T. Grant, "Fast Folk," *Harpers* (October 1979), pp. 106-110, satirically analyzes a woman in flight from intimacy in his discussion of a

Woman's Day heroine, Charlotte Soule, mother of two, ten-hour-a-day executive, and nightschool student, while her husband takes the children to school, prepares meals, shops, washes the clothes, and is also employed full-time. Grant concludes, rather waspishly, that "Charlotte Soule has overcome her fear of flying, but has she developed a fear of landing?" She and other such *fast folks* "are terrified of being truly biological and responsible human beings. . . . They neglect their obligations, but no one says so for fear of being considered unfashionable. They leave their kids in school year-round. They grant their children one quick kiss at bedtime. And *Woman's Day* magazine . . . *approves* of what they are doing." In such cases, my concern is with the children. Such parents procreate but choose not to nurture nor to be intimate.

23. Bronfenbrenner, "Context of Child Rearing," p. 22.

Chapter Six
Enduring Marriage:
The Illusion of Eroticism
The Reality of Complete Intimacy

1. Carol Tavris and Susan Sadd, *The Redbook Report on Female Sexuality* (New York: The Delacorte Press, 1977), p. 58.

2. W. Charles Lobitz and Gretchen K. Lobitz, "Clinical Assessment in the Treatment of Sexual Dysfunctions," in Joseph LoPiccolo and Leslie LoPiccolo, eds., *Handbook of Sex Therapy* (New York: Plenum Press, 1978), pp. 85-102. See also Helen F. Antonovsky, *Adolescent Sexuality* (Toronto: D. C. Heath and Company, 1980), p. 43.

3. As cited in Dorothy Marshall, *The Life and Times of Victoria* (New York: Praeger Publishers, 1972), pp. 120-21.

4. Marvin Harris, *Culture, Man and Nature* (New York: Thomas Y. Crowell Company, 1971), pp. 230-31.

5. A. Pietropinto and J. Simenauer, *Beyond the Male Myth* (New York: New York Times Book Company, 1977), p. 265.

6. *Ibid.*, p. 264.

7. Tavris and Sadd, *Redbook Report,* p. 37.

8. *Ibid.*, p. 54.

9. *Ibid.*, pp. 12-20.

10. *Ibid.*, p. 106.

11. Clifford H. Swensen, principal investigator, Charlotte Dickinson Moore, author, "Marriages that Endure," in NIMH monographs, *Families Today,* vol. 1, 1979, DHEW Publication no. (Adm) 79-815, pp. 249-88.

12. Cornelius Ryan and Kathryn Morgan Ryan, *A Private Battle* (New York: Fawcett Popular Library, 1979), pp. 212-14.

Afterword

1. Brooke Hayward, *Haywire* (New York: Knopf, Inc., 1977), pp. 367-68.

BIBLIOGRAPHIC COMMENTS AND REFERENCES

The popular and professional literature about human behavior is as diverse as the subjects it attempts to treat. A comprehensive bibliography would fill volumes and most selected bibliographies tend to focus on a certain discipline or ideology.

These comments and references are designed for those readers who wish to go beyond the notes but who realize that for each reference here, someone else might prefer another.

Those who adhere to strict scholarly literature object to popular references; I have used them occasionally since they often illustrate the trends of American society and the shape of our current culture. It is also important to realize that the popular magazines influence far more readers than professional journals, whose pages they mine and interpret.

Chapter One
The Illusions and Realities of Human Intimacy

Those interested in the demographic status of our society will wish to consult in greater detail those massive collections of raw data, the United States Bureau of the Census, *Statistical Abstract of the U.S.: 1978*, 99th ed., Washington, D.C., 1978. An extensive collection and interpretation of such data (though earlier) occurs in James S. Lynch, *The Broken Heart: The Medical Consequences of Loneliness* (New York: Basic Books, Inc., 1977).

The specific area of sex research has been dominated for the past decade by William H. Masters and Virginia E. Johnson, their works surpassing anything available at the time in clinical exploration and candid exposition. They include *Human Sexual Response* (Boston: Little, Brown and Company, 1966); *Human Sexual Inadequacy* (Boston: Little, Brown and Company, 1970); *Homosexuality in Perspective* (Boston: Little, Brown and Company, 1979); and *The Pleasure Bond*, a more popular work (New York: Little, Brown and Company, 1975). These researchers give previously unknown data on the physiologic processes of sexuality and offer therapy techniques for solving sexual dysfunction. However, they have come under critical attack because their reports leave out important items that would enable others to either replicate or evaluate their work. See Bernard Zilbergeld and Michael Evans, "The Inadequacy of Masters and Johnson," *Psychology Today,* August 1980, pp. 29-43 for some reasons why Masters and Johnson should not be accepted uncritically. Other critics have also noted internal inconsistencies, either in data or in conclusions, in their books, particularly when *The Pleasure Bond* is compared to *Homosexuality in Perspective.* Further, their attempts to be objective often lead to logically untenable avoidance of discussing consequences.

Helen Singer Kaplan, *The New Sex Therapy* (New York: Brunner/Mazel, 1974) and *Disorders of Sexual Desire* (New York: Brunner/Mazel, 1979), offers data similar to Masters and Johnson but extending beyond their work. However, she is more open with her data and methods and supplements laboratory work with counseling information. Her biological and drug data are especially valuable. Unfortunately, her strong bias against Judeo-Christian values colors her interpretations.

C. S. Lewis, novelist, Oxford and Cambridge lecturer, and Christian essayist, approaches human behavior from a theological perspective that is intensely concrete and practical. He has written so prolifically that one should consult a library listing to select from, and his entire work is strongly values-oriented whether he is writing a children's fairy tale (*The Lion, the Witch, and the Wardrobe*), science fiction (*Perelandra*), novels (*Till We Have Faces*), or essays (*Mere Christianity, The Problem of Pain,* and *Miracles*). Two very different works bear directly on the problem of human intimacy: *The Allegory of Love* (London: Oxford University Press, 1936) is literary criticism detailing the rise of "romantic" love in the Middle Ages; and *A Grief Observed* (New York: Bantam Books, 1976), the anguished journal he kept after his wife's death as he struggled to integrate the three realities of death, love, and faith.

The student seeking to understand modern mental health theory and practice is virtually obligated to begin with Sigmund Freud. His own works are available in several good translations and would be the best place to begin, but Frank J. Sulloway, *Freud: Biologist of the Mind* (New York: Basic Books, Inc., 1979), has performed a great service in sorting myth from fact and in providing information on the social and personal context in which those works were produced.

For a dispassionate and unbiased survey of current sex theories with their main practitioners, see Arno Karlen, *Sexuality and Homosexuality* (New York: W. W. Norton and Company, Inc., 1971). The same can be said about the balanced discussion of the consequences of divorce and, by extension, other intimate traumas, in Mavis Hetherington, "Divorce, a Child's Perspective," *American Psychologist* 34 (October 1979): 851-58.

A highly personal essay on the sources of significance under stress is Viktor Frankl, *Man's Search for Meaning* (New York: Pocket Books, 1963). He was one of several mental health professionals whose views were revised and tempered by personal suffering in a Nazi concentration camp during World War II. Bruno Bettleheim, *The Informed Heart* (New York: Avon Books, 1960), is another. Retrospective analysis from children whose parents survived the experience are recorded in Helen Epstein, *Children of the Holocaust* (New York: G. P. Putman's Sons, 1979). It may be beyond the power of language to describe either the loneliness or the intimacy that victims of the Holocaust experienced and that affected the lives of their offspring.

Another personal and autobiographical affirmation of Christian values coming out of World War II is Corrie ten Boom, *The Hiding Place* (New York: Bantam Books, 1971) and *Prison Letters* (New York: Bantam Books, 1979). In both cases, the test of concentration camp life exposed illusions and realities in the faith of Christian believers.

For those willing to take the time, perspective about human relationships over time are found in abundance throughout Will and Ariel Durant's *The Story of Civilization*, 10 vols. (New York: Simon and Schuster, 1954-1967).

To understand the difficulties in accurately recording human behavior, i.e., history, especially stimulating is Oscar Handlin's *Truth and History* (London: The Belknap Press of Harvard University, 1979).

In almost total methodological contrast but similar in their efforts to strike to the core of the human equation are books by Michael Polanyi, *Personal Knowledge: Towards a Post-Critical Philosophy* (Chicago: University of Chicago Press, 1962) and Studs Terkel, *Working* (New York: Pantheon Books, 1974) and *Hard Times* (New York: Pocket Books, 1970).

Other papers and essays on topics related to realities and illusions and intimacy include:

Altrocchi, John. *Abnormal Behavior*. New York: Harcourt-Brace-Jovanovich, Inc., 1980.

Apfelbaum, Bernard, "The Myth of the Surrogate." *The Journal of Sex Research* 13, no. 4 (1977), 238-49.

Ateyo, Don. *Blood and Guts: Violence in Sports*. London: Paddington Press, Ltd., 1979.

Bane, Mary Jo. "Marital Disruption and the Lives of Children." *Journal of Social Issues* 32, no. 1 (1976), 103-17.

Bell, Alan P., and Martin S. Weinberg. *Homosexualities: A Study of Diversity among Men and Women*. New York: Simon and Schuster, 1978.

Bennett, William J., "Simple Truths." *Newsweek* 7 January 1980, p. 7.

Bergin, Allen E., and Sol L. Garfield. *Handbook of Psychotherapy and Behavior Change*. New York: John Wiley and Sons, 1978.

___________. "Psychotherapy and Religious Values." *Journal of Consulting and Clinical Psychology* 48, no. 1 (1980), 95-105.

Bernstein, Barton E. "Legal and Social Interface in Counseling Homosexual Clients." *Social Casework* 58, no. 1 (January 1977), 36-40.

Cartwright, Frederick F., in collaboration with Michael D. Biddiss. *Disease and History*. New York: Thomas Y. Crowell Company, 1972.

Cohen, Eric J. "Holiness and Health: An Examination of the Relationship between Christian Holiness and Mental Health." *Journal of Psychology and Theology* 5, no. 4 (1977), 285-91.

Coleman, James C. *Abnormal Psychology and Modern Life*. 5th ed. Glenview, IL: Scott, Foresman and Company, 1976.

Csikszentmihalyi, Mihaly, and Ronald Graef. "Feeling Free." *Psychology Today* 13, no. 7 (December 1979), 84-85, 88, 90, 98-99.

Dictionary of Behavioral Science. Eds. Benjamin B. Wolman, et al. New York: Van Nostrand Reinhold Company, 1973.

Drucker, Peter F. *Adventures of a Bystander*. New York: Harper and Row Publishers, Inc., 1978.

Durant, Will, and Ariel Durant. *The Lessons of History*. New York: Simon and Schuster, 1968.

___________. *Rousseau and Revolution*, vol. 10 in *The Story of Civilization*. New York: Simon and Schuster, 1967.

Enstrom, James E. "CA/A Cancer Journal for Clinicians." *American Cancer Society* 29, no. 6 (November-December 1979), 352-61.

Feshbach, Seymour, and Neal Malamuth. "Sex and Aggression: Proving the Link." *Psychology Today* 12, no. 6 (November 1978), 110-12, 114, 116, 117, 122.

Forster-Nietzsche, Frau. *The Lonely Nietzsche*. Trans. Paul V. Cohen. London: W. Heinemann, 1915.

Freedman, Jonathan L. *Introductory Psychology*. Reading, MA: Addison-Wesley Publishing Company, 1978.

Freedman, Alfred M., Harold I. Kaplan, and Benjamin J. Sadock, eds. *Comprehensive Textbook of Psychiatry/II*. 2nd ed. Baltimore: The Williams and Wilkins Company, 1975, vol. 2.

French, Anthony Phillip, ed. *Einstein: A Centenary Volume*. Cambridge: Harvard University Press, 1979.

Freud, Sigmund. "A Letter from Freud." *The American Journal of Psychiatry* 107 (1951), 786-87.

___________. *Standard Edition of the Complete Psychological Works*. 24 vols. London: Hogarth Press and the Institute of Psycho-Analysis, 1964.

Gebhard, Paul H., et al. *Sex Offenders*. New York: Harper and Row, 1965.

Grant, Michael. *Jesus: An Historian's Review of the Gospels.* New York: Charles Scribner's Sons, 1978.

Groth, A. Nicholas. *Men Who Rape.* New York: Plenum Press, 1979.

Hayward, Brooke. *Haywire.* Toronto: Bantam Books, 1978.

Hollander, L. M., trans. *Selections from the Writings of Kierkegaard.* Garden City, NY: Doubleday and Company, 1960.

Kaplan, Helen Singer. *Disorders of Sexual Desire.* New York: Brunner/Mazel, Inc., 1979.

____________. *The New Sex Therapy.* New York: Brunner/Mazel, Inc., 1974.

Keen, Sam. "Another Style of Valor—Emotional Risk and Commitment." *Self,* November 1979, pp. 59-60.

Kenyon, Karen. "A Survivor's Notes." *Newsweek* 30 April 1979, p. 17.

Klass, Ellen Tobey. "Psychological Effects of Immoral Actions: The Experimental Evidence." *Psychological Bulletin* 85, no. 4 (1978), 765-71.

Kohn, Melvin L. *Class and Conformity: A Study in Values.* 2nd ed. Chicago: The University of Chicago Press, 1977.

Kottak, C. P. *Anthropology: The Exploration of Human Diversity.* New York: Random House, 1974.

Lapham, Lewis H. "A Juggernaut of Words." *Harpers* June 1979, pp. 8-16.

Lasch, Christopher. *The Culture of Narcissism.* New York: W. W. Norton and Company, Inc., 1979.

Lazarus, Richard S. "Positive Denial: The Case for Not Facing Reality." *Psychology Today* 13, no. 6 (November 1979), 44-60.

Logan, Joshua. *Movie Stars, Real People and Me.* New York: Delacorte Press, 1978.

Lowenfeld, Henry, and Yela Lowenfeld. "Our Permissive Society and the Superego." *Psychoanalytic Quarterly* 39, no. 4 (1970), 590-608.

Madsen, Truman G. *Christ and the Inner Life.* Salt Lake City: Bookcraft, 1978.

____________. "Philosophy and the Public Policy." *The Humanities and Public Policy.* Utah Endowment for the Humanities (n.d.).

Maugh, Thomas H., II. "Cancer and Environment: Higginson Speaks Out." *Science* 205, no. 4413 (28 September 1979), 1363-64, 1366.

Menninger, Karl. *Whatever Became of Sin?* New York: Hawthorn Books, Inc., 1973.

Millar, T. P. "Who's Afraid of Sigmund Freud?" *British Journal of Psychiatry* 115 (1969), 421-28.

Moan, Charles E., and Robert G. Heath. "Septal Stimulation for the Initiation of Heterosexual Behavior in a Homosexual Male." *Journal of Behavior Therapy and Experimental Psychiatry* 3 (1972), 23-30.

Money, John, and Anke Ehrhardt. *Man and Woman, Boy and Girl.* Baltimore: The Johns Hopkins University Press, 1972.

Morrow, Lance. "Back to Reticence." *Time* 4 February 1980, p. 86.

Oregon (state), Department of Human Resources. *Final Report of the Task Force on Sexual Preference.* Portland, December 1, 1978.

Solzhenitsyn, Aleksandr. "A World Split Apart." *Vital Speeches of the Day* 45, no. 22 (September 1978), 678-84.

____________. *The Gulag Archipelago.* Trans. Thomas P. Whitney. New York: Harper and Row Publishers, Inc., 1974.

Steinmetz, Urban G. *The Sexual Christian.* St. Meinrad, IN: Abbey Press, 1972.

Sutherland, Norman S. *Breakdown: A Personal Crisis and a Medical Dilemma.* London: Weidenfeld and Nicolson, 1976.

Teichmann, Howard. *George S. Kaufman: An Intimate Portrait.* New York: Atheneum, 1972.

Twombly, Wells. *200 Years of Sport in America.* New York: McGraw-Hill Book Company, 1976.

U.S. Bureau of the Census. *Statistical Abstract of the U.S.: 1978.* 99th ed. Washington, D.C., 1978.

Varela, Jacob A. "Solving Human Problems with Human Science." *Human Nature* October 1978, pp. 84-90.

Wallace, Anthony F. "Detailed Reservations Regarding the Task Force Recommendations on Social Policy." In J. M. Livingood, ed., *National Institute of Mental Health Task Force on Homosexuality: Final Report and Background Papers.* Rockville, MD: U.S. Department of Health, Education, and Welfare. Publ. no. (HSM) 72-9119, 1972, p. 71.

Weinberg, George H. *Society and the Healthy Homosexual.* New York: St. Martin's Press, 1972.

Will, George F. "A Right to Health." *Newsweek* 7 August 1978, p. 88.

Wolman, Benjamin B., ed. *Handbook of General Psychology.* Englewood Cliffs, NJ: Prentice-Hall, Inc., 1973.

Chapter Two
The Reality of Identity

Child development is both blessed by and suffers from an abundance of literature. I have frequently recommended that parents avoid too much reliance upon this part of the literature because they tend to lose confidence in their own ability and judgment. However, an author who respects parents is Burton L. White, *The First Three Years of Life* (Englewood Cliffs, NJ: Prentice-Hall, 1975) and *A Parent's Guide to the First Three Years* (Englewood Cliffs, NJ: Prentice-Hall, 1980).

Alice S. Rossi, "A Biosocial Perspective on Parenting," *Daedalus* 106 (Spring 1977): 1-31; and her "Materialism, Sexuality, and the New Feminism" in Joseph Zubin and John Money, eds., *Contemporary Sexual Behavior* (Baltimore: Johns Hopkins University Press, 1973), examines children and identity from her orientation as a women's rights activist who highly values nurturant motherhood.

For wisdom and perspective any reader would and should benefit from Erik H. Erickson, *Childhood and Society*, 2nd ed. rev. (New York: W. W. Norton and Company, 1963).

Journal articles and other reference works on early childhood development are:

Beach, Frank A. ed. *Human Sexuality in Four Perspectives.* Baltimore: The Johns Hopkins University Press, 1977.

Bettelheim, Bruno. *The Uses of Enchantment.* New York: Vintage Books, 1977.

Bowen, Murray. "Toward the Differentiation of Self in One's Family of Origin." *Georgetown Family Symposium Papers*, vol. 1. Eds. F. Andres and J. Lorio. Washington, D.C.: Georgetown University Press, 1974, pp. 70-86.

Bower, T. G. R. *Infant Development.* San Francisco: W. H. Freeman and Co., 1977.

Bronfenbrenner, Urie. "Contexts of Child Rearing: Problems and Prospects." *American Psychologist* 34, no. 10 (1979), 844-50.

Chodoff, Paul. "A Critique of Freud's Theory of Infantile Sexuality." *The American Journal of Psychiatry* 123, no. 5 (1966), 507-18.

Cohen, Yehudi. "The Disappearance of the Incest Taboo." *Human Nature* July 1978, pp. 72-78.

Craig, Grace J. *Child Development.* Englewood Cliffs, NJ: Prentice-Hall, Inc., 1979.

DeMott, Benjamin. "The Pro-Incest Lobby." *Psychology Today* 13, no. 10 (March 1980), 11-16.

Framo, James L. "Family of Origin as a Therapeutic Resource for Adults in Marital and Family Therapy: You Can and Should Go Home Again." *Family Process* 15, no. 2 (1976), 193-210.

Gagnon, John H. "Sexuality and Sexual Learning in the Child." *Psychiatry* 28 (1965), 212-28.

Garmezy, Norman. "Vulnerable and Invulnerable Children: Theory, Research, and Intervention." *Journal Supplement Abstract Service*, MS 1337.

Hall, Calvin S., and Gardner Lindzey. *Theories of Personality.* New York: John Wiley and Sons, Inc., 1970.

Henley, Arthur. *Demon in My View.* New York: Trident Press, 1966.

Kagan, Jerome, and Robert E. Klein. "Cross-Cultural Perspectives on Early Development." *American Psychologist* 28, no. 11 (1973), 947-61.

____________, Richard B. Kearsley, and Philip R. Zelazo. *Infancy: Its Place in Human Development.* Cambridge: Harvard University Press, 1978.

____________. "The Baby's Elastic Mind." *Human Nature* January 1978, pp. 66-73.

Lamb, Michael E. *The Role of the Father in Child Development.* New York: John Wiley and Sons, 1976.

Landreth, Catherine. *Early Childhood: Behavior and Learning.* New York: Alfred A. Knopf, Inc., 1967.

Lewinska, Pelagia. *Twenty Months at Auschwitz.* New York: Lyle Stuart, Inc., 1968.

Lewis, Michael, and Leonard A. Rosenblum, eds. *The Effect of the Infant on Its Caregiver.* New York: John Wiley and Sons, Inc., 1974.

Maslow, Abraham H. *Motivation and Personality.* New York: Harper and Row Publishers, 1954.

Mischel, Walter. "How Children Postpone Pleasure." *Human Nature* December 1978, pp. 51-55.

Monge, R. H. "Structure of the Self-Concept from Adolescence through Old-Age." *Experimental Aging Research* 1, no. 2 (1975), 281-91.

Pines, Maya. "Superkids." *Psychology Today* 12, no. 8 (January 1979), pp. 53-63.

Skolnick, Arlene. "The Myth of the Vulnerable Child." *Psychology Today* 11, no. 9 (February 1978), 56-60, 65.

Spitz, Rene A. "Hospitalism. An Inquiry into the Genesis of Psychiatric Conditions in Early Childhood." *Psychoanalytic Study of the Child* 1 (1945), 53-74.

Spock, Benjamin. *Baby and Child Care.* New York: Hawthorn Books, Inc., 1968.

Stevens, Joseph H., Jr., and Marilyn Mathews. *Mother/Child Father/Child Relationships.* Washington, D.C.: National Association for the Education of Young Children, 1978.

White, Theodore. *In Search of History: A Personal Adventure.* New York: Harper and Row Publishers, 1978.

Williamson, Donald S. "New Life at the Graveyard: A Method of Therapy for Individuation from a Dead Former Parent." *The Journal of Marriage and Family Counseling* 4, no. 1 (1978), 93-101.

Chapter Three
The Illusion of Stereotypes
The Reality of Roles

A father's influence upon his children's role development has been neglected until recently. Michael E. Lamb has surveyed the literature helpfully in

The Role of the Father in Child Development (New York: John Wiley and Sons, 1976). Psychological insights are found in various articles by George A. Rekers including "Atypical Gender Development and Psychosocial Adjustment," *Journal of Applied Behavior Analysis* 10 (1977): 559-71.

An interesting book which recounts both the strength and the superficiality of roles under stress in a Japanese prison camp is Langdon Gilkey's *Shantung Compound* (New York: Harper and Row, 1966).

For data on biological-psychological role and gender factors, the work of John Money and Anke Ehrhardt is very valuable. See their *Man and Woman, Boy and Girl* (Baltimore: The Johns Hopkins University Press, 1972).

Any basic sociology text will discuss roles and any basic cultural anthropology text is helpful in understanding the cultural origin and reinforcement of roles.

Related periodical and journal articles that are also helpful include:

Barlow, David H., Gene G. Abel, and Edward B. Blanchard. "Gender Identity Change in Transsexuals." *Archives of General Psychiatry* 36 (1979), 1001-1007.

Beals, Ralph L., and Harry Hoijer. *An Introduction to Anthropology* (New York: The Macmillan Company, 1959).

Beit-Hallahmi, Benjamin, and Albert I. Rabin. "The Kibbutz as a Social Experiment and as a Child-Rearing Laboratory." *American Psychologist* 32, no. 7 (1977), 532-41.

Bem, Sandra L. "Sex Role Adaptability: One Consequence of Psychological Androgyny." *Journal of Personality and Social Psychology* 31, no. 4 (1975), 634-43.

___________. "The Measurement of Psychological Androgyny." *Journal of Consulting and Clinical Psychology* 42, no. 2 (1974), 155-62.

Bergman, B. R., and I. Adelman. "The 1973 Report of the President's Council of Economic Advisers: The Economic Role of Women." *The American Economic Review* 63, no. 4 (1973), 509-14.

Boston Women's Health Book Collective. *Our Bodies, Ourselves: A Book by and for Women.* Rev. 2nd ed. New York: Simon and Schuster, 1975.

Broom, Leonard, and Philip Selznick. *Sociology.* New York: Harper and Row, 1963.

Dreyer, Albert S., Valerie Hulac, and David Rigler. "Differential Adjustment to Pubescence and Cognitive Style Patterns." *Development Psychology* 4, no. 3 (1971), 456-62.

Friedl, Ernestine. "Society and Sex Roles." *Human Nature* April 1978, pp. 68-75.

Frieze, Irene H., et al. *Woman and Sex Roles.* New York: W. W. Norton and Company, 1978.

Goffman, Erving. *Gender Advertisements.* Cambridge: Harvard University Press, 1979.

Gold, Dolores, and David Andres. "Developmental Comparisons between Ten-

Year-Old Children with Employed and Non-employed Mothers." *Child Development* 49, no. 1 (March 1978), 75-84.

Grant, Louis T. "Fast Folk." *Harpers,* October 1979, pp. 106-10.

Harris, Marvin. *Culture, Man and Nature: An Introduction to General Anthropology.* New York: Thomas Y. Crowell Company, 1971.

Hoffman, Lois Wladis. "Maternal Employment: 1979." *American Psychologist* 34, no. 10 (1979), 859-65.

Imperato-McGinley, Julianne, et al. "Androgens and the Evolution of Male-Gender Identity among Male Pseudohermaphrodites with 5-Reductase Deficiency." *New England Journal of Medicine* 300, no. 22 (1979), 1233-37.

Kandel, Denise B. "Homophyly, Selections and Socialization in Adolescents." *American Journal of Sociology* 84 (September 1978), 427-36.

Koedt, Anne, Ellen Levine, and Anita Rapone, eds. *Radical Feminism.* New York: Time Books, 1973.

Leiderman, P. Herbert, Steven R. Tulkin, and Anne Rosenfeld. *Culture and Infancy.* New York: Academic Press, Inc., 1977.

Levy, David M. *Maternal Overprotection.* New York: Columbia University Press, 1943.

Lloyd, Scott. "Is the Woman's Place Really in the Home?" *BYU Today* December 1979, pp. 11-12.

Maccoby, Eleanor E. "Sex Differentiation during Childhood." *Journal Supplement Abstract Service.* MS 1339.

Mead, Margaret. *Male and Female.* New York: William Morrow and Company, Publishers, 1949.

Meyer, Jon K., and Donna J. Reter. "Sex Reassignment: Follow-up." *Archives of General Psychiatry* 36 (1979), 1010-15.

Miller, William, as told to Frances S. Leighton. *Fishbait.* Englewood Cliffs, NJ: Prentice-Hall, Inc., 1977.

Money, John, and Duane Alexander. "Eroticism and Sexual Function in Developmental Anorchia and Hyporchia with Pubertal Failure." *The Journal of Sex Research* 3, no. 1 (February 1967), 31-47.

Pixa, Bea. "Talking to Women about the Rest of Their Lives." *San Francisco Sunday Examiner and Chronicle* 30 September 1979, p. Scene 5.

Shostak, Marjorie. "Memories of a Kung Girlhood." *Human Nature* June 1978, pp. 80-88.

Spencer, Meta. *Foundations of Modern Sociology.* Englewood Cliffs, NJ: Prentice-Hall, Inc., 1976.

Spiro, Melford E. *Gender and Culture: Kibbutz Women Revisited.* Durham, NC: Duke University Press, 1979.

Tavris, Carol, and Carole Offir. *The Longest War: Sex Differences in Perspective.* New York: Harcourt-Brace-Jovanovich, Inc., 1977.

"The Nation's New Schoolmistress." *Newsweek* 12 November 1979, p. 41.

Wells, Kathleen. "Gender-Role Identity and Psychological Adjustment in Adolescence." New York, September 1979. (Paper presented at the American Psychological Association.)

Chapter Four
The Illusion of Sexual Exploitation
The Reality of Relationship Skills

Here the reader is obliged to read widely and with careful discrimination. Many authors make the fundamental mistake of confusing sexual intimacy with nonsexual intimacy. Thus, the student of behavior must resign himself to a journey through widely differing, frequently contradictory points of view. Biography, autobiography, and history are helpful because, though seldom objective, they permit human lives to be scrutinized in the same way that case studies can sometimes bring pertinent facts to light.

Alfred C. Kinsey, Wardell B. Pomeroy, and Clyde E. Martin, *Sexual Behavior in the Human Male* (Philadelphia: W. B. Saunders Company, 1948) and Alfred C. Kinsey, et al, *Sexual Behavior in the Human Female* (New York: Pocket Books, 1965), are important, primarily because they are unique early studies. They are badly flawed due to research error and are not reliable bases for value interpretations. But since modern sexual research begins there, the serious student must be acquainted with them, not only for their information but to understand how tenuous, though earnest, are the foundations of modern "sexology."

Dorothy R. Blitsten, *The World of the Family* (New York: Random House, 1963), offers an anthropological review of the various ways nuclear and extended families experience relationships.

For basic description and achievements of identity, role, and relationships, the life of Helen Keller and her companion-teacher is unsurpassed and is thoroughly examined in Joseph P. Lash, *Helen and Teacher: The Story of Helen Keller and Anne Sullivan Macy* (New York: Delacorte Press/Seymour Lawrence, 1980).

Other books and articles researching relationships and human sexuality include:

Allen, Gina, and Clement G. Martin. *Intimacy: Sensitivity, Sex, and the Art of Love.* Chicago: Cowles Book Company, Inc., 1971.

Arieti, Silvano, and Jules Bemporad. *Severe and Mild Depression.* New York: Basic Books, Inc., 1978.

Bandura, Albert. "The Stormy Decade: Fact or Fiction." *Psychology in the Schools* 1, no. 3 (July 1964), 224-31.

Bensman, Joseph, and Robert Lilienfeld. "Friendship and Alienation." *Psychology Today* 13, no. 4 (October 1979), 56-57, 59, 60, 63, 66, 114.

Bergin, Allen E. "A Self-Regulation Technique for Impulse Control Disorders." *Psychotherapy: Theory, Research and Practice* 6 (1969), 113-118.

Bettelheim, Bruno. *The Informed Heart: Autonomy in a Mass Age.* New York: Avon Books, 1960.

Brecher, Ruth, and Edward Brecher. *An Analysis of Human Sexual Response.* New York: The New American Library, Inc., 1966.

Davison, G. C. "Elimination of a Sadistic Fantasy by a Client-Controlled Counterconditioning Technique." *Journal of Abnormal Psychology* 73, no. 1 (1968), 84-90.

Fromm, Erich. *The Heart of Man: Its Genius for Good and Evil.* New York: Harper and Row, 1964.

Hardy, Kenneth R. "An Appetitional Theory of Sexual Motivation." *Psychological Review* 71, no. 1 (1964), 1-18.

Hunt, Richard A., and Morton B. King. "Religiousity and Marriage." *Journal for the Scientific Study of Religion* 17, no. 4 (1978), 399-406.

Hutchison, J. B., ed. *Biological Determinants of Sexual Behavior.* New York: John Wiley and Sons, 1978.

Katchadourian, Herant A., and Donald T. Lunde. *Fundamentals of Human Sexualism.* New York: Hold, Rinehart and Winston, 1975.

Kernberg, Otto F. *Borderline Conditions and Pathological Narcissism.* New York: Jason Aronson, Inc., 1975.

Kinsey, Alfred Charles, et al. *Sexual Behavior in the Human Female.* New York: Pocket Books, Inc., 1965.

____________, Wardell B. Pomeroy, and Clyde E. Martin. *Sexual Behavior in the Human Male.* Philadelphia: W. B. Saunders Company, 1948.

Levin, Adeline L., and Beatrice H. Lynch. *Human Sexuality in Family Life Education.* Dubuque, IA. Kendall/Hunt Publishing Company, 1976.

LoPiccolo, Joseph, and Leslie LoPiccolo, eds. *Handbook of Sex Therapy.* New York: Plenum Press, 1978.

McGuire, R. J., J. M. Carlisle, and B. G. Young. "Sexual Deviations as Conditioned Behavior: A Hypothesis." *Behavior Research and Therapy* 2 (1965), 185-90.

Peck, M. Scott. *The Road Less Traveled.* New York: Simon and Schuster, 1978.

Sarnoff, Suzanne, and Irving Sarnoff. *Sexual Excitement, Sexual Peace.* New York: M. Evans and Co., Inc., 1979.

Sommer, Barbara B. *Puberty and Adolescence.* New York: Oxford University Press, 1978.

Tiefer, Leonore. "The Kiss." *Human Nature* July 1978, pp. 28-37.

Whyte, William Foote. *Street Corner Society.* Chicago: University of Chicago Press, 1955.

Wilson, Beclee Newcomer. "Human Sexuality and Interpersonal Communication: An Exploration." *Counseling and Values* 23, no. 2 (February 1979), 73-81.

Yochelson, Samuel, and Stanton E. Samenow. *The Criminal Personality, Volume I: A Profile for Change.* New York: Jason Aronson, 1976.

____________. *The Criminal Personality, Volume II: The Change Process.* New York: Jason Aronson, 1977.

Zubin, Joseph, and John Money, eds. *Contemporary Sexual Behavior.* Baltimore: The Johns Hopkins University Press, 1973.

Chapter Five
Beginning Marriage: The Illusion of Cohabitation The Reality of Homebuilding

Few topics are treated more frequently or more superficially than the American family, particularly in popular magazines. As with literature on relationships, information about the family is gathered in segments after diligent searching. James Lynch's *The Broken Heart: Medical Consequences of Loneliness* (New York: Basic Books, 1977) examines companionship both sociologically and psychologically and provides an able interpretation of the consequences of married versus unmarried life in the 1970s. Lewis A. Coser, *The Functions of Social Conflict* (Glencoe, IL: The Free Press, 1956), is one of those little books that is both valuable and a bit dull, but offers a perspective for the inevitable clashes within intimate relationships.

Students of our culture and its values are numerous. I have found Christopher Lasch, *The Culture of Narcissism* (New York: W. W. Norton and Co., 1979), particularly valuable for his psycho-social history of the Western (especially the American) obsession with self.

Damage done by narrow preoccupation with the nuclear family model is discussed by Azubike Felix Uzoka in "The Myth of the Nuclear Family," *American Psychologist,* November 1979, pp. 1095-1106.

Carol Tavris and Susan Sadd, *The Redbook Report on Female Sexuality* (New York: The Delacorte Press, 1977), offer a wider view of intimacy than is usually found in research-based books. William J. Lederer and Don D. Jackson, *The Mirages of Marriage* (New York: W. W. Norton and Company, 1968), appraise marriage but often with pessimism.

From his widower's sorrow, Sheldon Vanauken, *A Severe Mercy* (San Francisco: Harper and Row Publishers, 1977), shares the beginning and ending of his marriage.

Anne Morrow Lindbergh has opened to the reader very private experiences in her several books. Among these are: *Hour of Gold, Hour of Lead* (New York: Harcourt-Brace-Jovanovich, 1973), the account of their baby's kidnapping and death; *War Within and Without* (New York: Harcourt-Brace-Jovanovich, 1980), an account of her husband Charles's struggles; *Gift from the Sea* (New York: Pantheon, 1955), a woman's reflections on intimacy.

The beginnings and endurance of the Churchills' long marriage is instructive and fascinating as told in Mary Soames, *Clementine Churchill: The Biography of a Marriage* (Boston: Houghton Mifflin Company, 1979).

Becoming a parent is the variable which most powerfully affects beginning marriage. An enjoyable and informative book is *A Reader for Parents,* ed. The Child Study Association of America (New York: W. W. Norton and Company, Inc., 1963).

Other helpful references include:

Boszormenyi-Nagy, Ivan, and Geraldine M. Spark. *Invisible Loyalties.* Hagerstown, MD: Medical Department, Harper and Row Publishers, Inc., 1973.

Bowen, Murray. *Family Therapy in Clinical Practice.* New York: Jason Aronson, 1978.

Bronfenbrenner, Urie. "The Disturbing Changes in the American Family." *Education Digest,* 42, no. 6 (February 1977), 22-25.

Campbell, Donald. "On the Conflicts between Biological and Social Evolution and between Psychology and Moral Tradition." *American Psychologist* 30, no. 12 (1975), 1102-26.

Cherlin, Andrew. "Cohabitation: How the French and Swedes Do It." *Psychology Today* 13, no. 4 (October 1979), 18, 24.

Gardner, Richard A. *Psychotherapy with Children of Divorce.* Garden City, NY: Doubleday and Company, 1977.

Gettleman, Susan, and Janet Markowitz. *The Courage to Divorce.* New York: Simon and Schuster, 1974.

Gilbert Neil. "An Initial Agenda for Family Policy." *Social Work* 24, no. 6 (1979), 447-50.

Homans, George C. *The Human Group.* New York: Harcourt, Brace and World, Inc., 1950).

Mancini, Jay A., and Dennis K. Orthner. "Recreational Sexuality Preferences among Middle-Class Husbands and Wives." *The Journal of Sex Research* 14, no. 2 (May 1978), 96-106.

Manosevitz, Martin. "Early Sexual Behavior in Adult Homosexual and Heterosexual Males." *Journal of Abnormal Psychology* 76, no. 3 (1970), 396-402.

Money, John, ed. *Sex Research: New Developments.* New York: Holt, Rinehart and Winston, 1965.

Mudd, Emily H., Maurice J. Karpf, Abraham Stone, Janet Fowler Nelson. *Marriage Counseling: A Casebook.* New York: Association Press, 1958.

Rogers, Dorothy. *The Adult Years: An Introduction to Aging.* Englewood Cliffs, NJ: Prentice-Hall, Inc., 1979.

Symons, Donald. *The Evolution of Human Sexuality.* New York: Oxford University Press, 1979.

Tavris, Carol, and Susan Sadd. *The Redbook Report on Female Sexuality.* New York: The Delacorte Press, 1977.

Wallerstein, Judith S., and Joan B. Kelly. "Children and Divorce: A Review." *Social Work* 24, no. 6 (1979), 468-75.

Washburn, S. L. "What We Can't Learn about People from Apes." *Human Nature* November 1978, pp. 70-75.

Chapter Six: Enduring Marriage: The Illusion of Eroticism The Reality of Complete Intimacy

Erik H. Erikson's *Childhood and Society* is valuable here as well as in a previous chapter for a study of early childhood as he places the stages of life in a framework of insightful common sense. For a relaxed visit with this wise man see also Richard I. Evans, *Dialogue with Erik Erikson* (New York: Harper and Row, 1967). Again Carol Tavris and Susan Sadd, The *Redbook Report on Female Sexuality* (New York: The Delacorte Press, 1977), go beyond the usual erotic details and gather information about female views of marriage at various stages. A. Pietropinto and J. Simenauer, *Beyond the Male Myth* (New York: New York Times Book Company, 1977), offer similar though limited data. Robert R. Sears, "Sources of Life Satisfactions of the Terman Gifted Men," *American Psychologist,* 32 (1977): 119-28, gives helpful insight into lives over time in the developing values and lifestyles of an important group of gifted male children in the first part of the twentieth century. Clifford H. Swensen, principal investigator, Charlotte Dickinson Moore, author, "Marriages that Endure," in *Families Today,* NIMH Monographs I (1979): 79-815, have undertaken the important task of studying marriages over time in the last part of the twentieth century.

The strength of a mature marriage is seen in the account of one spouse's death in Cornelius Ryan and Kathryn Morgan Ryan, *A Private Battle* (New York: Simon and Schuster, 1979).

Other studies include:

Antonovsky, Helen F. *Adolescent Sexuality.* Toronto: D. C. Heath and Company, 1980.

Ard, Ben N., Jr. "Sex in Lasting Marriages: A Longitudinal Study." *The Journal of Sex Research* 13, no. 4 (1977), 274-85.

Broderick, Carlfred. *Couples.* New York: Simon and Schuster, 1979.

Busse, Ewald, and Eric Pfeiffer, eds. *Behavior and Adaptation in Late Life.* Boston: Little, Brown and Company, 1969.

____________. *Mental Illness in Later Life.* Washington D.C.: American Psychiatric Association, 1973.

Byrd, Richard E. *Alone.* New York: G. P. Putnam's Sons, 1938.

Cannon, Kenneth L. *Developing a Marriage Relationship.* Provo, UT: Brigham Young University Press, 1972.

Erikson, Erik H., ed. *Adulthood.* New York: W. W. Norton and Company, Inc., 1978.

Gann, Ernest K. *A Hostage to Fortune.* New York: Alfred A. Knopf, 1978.

Goldman, Ralph, and Morris Rockstein, eds. *The Physiology and Pathology of Human Aging.* New York: Academic Press, Inc., 1975.

Hall, G. Stanley. *Senescence: The Last Half of Life.* New York: D. Appleton and Company, 1922.

Hawthorne, Julian. *Nathaniel Hawthorne and His Wife.* Vol. 1. 1884; rpt. Hamden, CT: Archon Books, 1968.

Kunhardt, Philip B., Jr. *My Father's House.* New York: Random House, 1970.

Maguire, Marjorie Reiley. "The Ultimate Value Question." *Counseling and Values* 22, no. 7 (July 1978), 273-78.

Nash, John. *Developmental Psychology.* 2nd ed. Englewood Cliffs, NJ: Prentice-Hall, Inc., 1978.

Neugarten, Bernice L. "The Psychology of Aging: An Overview." *Journal Supplement Abstract Service,* MS 1340.

Novak, Michael. "The Family Out of Favor." *Harpers* April 1976, pp. 37-46.

Schaar, Karen. "Vermont: Getting through the Adult Years." *APA Monitor,* September-October 1978, pp. 7, 29, 34.

Vischer, A. L. *On Growing Old.* Boston: Houghton Mifflin Company, 1967.

Waller, Willard. *The Old Love and The New: Divorce and Readjustment.* Carbondale, IL: Southern Illinois University Press, 1967.

Williams, Richard H., and Claudine G. Wirths. *Lives through the Years.* New York: Atherton Press, 1965.

____________, Clark Tibbits, and Wilma Donahue, eds. *Processes of Aging.* 2 vols. New York: Atherton Press, 1963.

INDEX

-U-

-V-

-W-